The Political and Social thought of John Richard Spencer

A nonviolent anarchist

Political and social essays of John Spencer
Politics, Society and Life

TABLE OF CONTENTS

Foreword 5

"1984" is coming sooner than you thought 6

American gun massacres and the 2nd Amendment 9

Be Afraid of the Future 11

The only real solution to the Refugee Crisis 11

Why the world's economic system destroys people 12

Beyond Good and Evil 14

Artificial Intelligence-the way forward or the precursor to
the doom of humanity? 15

Hitler and Jesus were both right 18

Are the ever-increasing financial complexities of the
contemporary world destroying your peace of mind? 19

Environment, Society and Economy 23

The Singularity ....

Brexit-Like a bitter, expensive and unnecessary divorce
where everybody loses 24

Julian Assange-champion of Freedom and Transparency 26

Populism, short-sightedness and the height of Folly 30

The Evil Triangle of World Power 34

China's uncompromising plan to take over much of the world 36

Theresa May's Brexit Obsession as a recipe for disaster 37

The UK and Europe at the Crossroads 38

Vladimir Putin's War on the West 42

What the rise of China, Putin's Russia and Brexit mean for freedom 44

Islamist Jihad, Freedom and Human Rights 49
Beliefs in themselves 50
Actions and the Rights of Others 51
The Rights of Refugees 52
Capitalism, War and the Arab Spring 54
War and Capitalism 55
Recep Tayip Erdoğan 57
Were Nazi Economics the Real Cause of WWII? 59
The Brexit Debacle 61
Leaders the World would be better off without 62
A realistic Charter of human rights 73
The Global Corona virus pandemic and
   its aftermath – What will follow? 77
Australia and the PRC Chinese Diaspora 80
The Expansion of China and the rise of Covid-19 virus 84

Essays about Humanity and Lifestyle 92

A Metaphor for Humanity 93
Testosterone and Youth 94
Healthy attitudes to sex go a long way towards a Healthy Society 95
The World spends more of its scare resources on prolonging
   the lives of the frail elderly, many of whom are in a
   terminal condition, than it does on promoting the
   health of babies and young children 98
Early Demise for the Elderly 103
Buddhism and Christianity 106
Tobacco taxes, poverty and organised crime 107
Want to be rich for a day or a month? 110

Addendum promoting novel, "Brownout-666; the Inside Story of a Misguided life in the drug and sex trade and the Real Meaning of the Swastika p. 195

Foreword

(July 2020)

The following essays and blog posts have been written over several years. I have tried to place them in such a way as to make a consistent thread. Therefore, to that end, they are not simply placed in date order but are grouped to a large extent by subject. I have placed the approximate date next to each post so that the reader can understand if the post refers to world leaders and events that have been overtaken by subsequent history.

All photographs and artwork, unless otherwise attributed, have been taken from the public domain or belong to the author.

ଚ ♦ ♦ ♦ ♦ ଓ

"1984" is coming sooner than you thought

Privacy, Security and Freedom

(Feb 2015)

(from Google images)

Since the recent whistle-blowing of Edward Snowden there has been a huge interest in the USA and elsewhere on the questions of Privacy, Freedom and Security and the price for each. The fact that these questions are even being asked reflects poorly on the intelligence and education of the common man. Privacy, Freedom and Security are all very relative concepts. In absolute terms there is no real freedom in the world and never has been. The freedom of every one of us has always been constrained by natural limitations and the freedoms of others. No-one and nothing is ever really free! Similarly, there is no real security. We are all subject to the vagaries of Fate!

As to privacy, that may once have existed to a considerable extent but anyone in the modern world who believes that we still have any serious degree of it is a fool. It is possible to find out almost anything about anyone. Many politicians and famous people have learned this to their detriment. It was different in the times of Abraham Lincoln and John F. Kennedy. In the contemporary world the technological sophistication of spying techniques is such that none of us have any real privacy anyway. At present, at least our thoughts are our own but how long that will last is anyone's guess.

(from Google images)

If people believe that their details remain at all private in this electronic age they are totally deluded. Some police forces have number plate detection cameras atop their cars that record every vehicle they pass such that everywhere that vehicle has been for years, (and presumably that vehicle's owner in most cases,) can be extracted from a database.

Our smart phones enable enough data about our movements, history, life preferences and politics to be grabbed by governments and companies to fill volumes. Scores of shopping centres around the world are extracting data from such phones and sending it who knows where? Much of the data ends up in the USA, which possibly has some constitutional protections for its own citizens but none for the rest of us.

"WHO CONTROLS THE PAST
CONTROLS THE FUTURE
WHO CONTROLS THE PRESENT
CONTROLS THE PAST"

(from Google images)

If that isn't enough our use of Facebook (and other social media) give governments even more information about ourselves to fill in any gaps in their knowledge. Doubtless, my views expressed in this blog have been collected somewhere by various government authorities. However, I am probably too insignificant for those bodies to be concerned by them.

Edward Snowden's revelations caused considerable protest against US spying by governments in Europe and elsewhere. Unsurprisingly, the Australian government along with both major political parties said nothing. It just hoped that the public would forget about it quickly.

Unfortunately, democracy is only as good as its Lowest Common Denominator. That translates as "democratic governments reflect the values and attitudes of the lowest level of their citizens where that lowest level boasts the largest numbers."

(from Google images)

It would seem certain that the power brokers of our planet will destroy the environment and any semblance of a decent society at the same time as politically destroying the last vestiges of human freedom. In his vision of the future the only thing that George Orwell got wrong was the date!

The coming world will much more resemble *"1984"* than Aldous Huxley's one portrayed in *"Brave New World,"* as in the latter vision the populace at least were given drugs to keep them content. Our world wants to tax or remove any chemical help and leave control by war and terror.

American gun massacres and the 2nd Amendment

(Mar 2018)

George Washington
(from Google images)

Andrew Jackson
(from Google images)

When the founding fathers of the U.S. constitution framed the Second Amendment, they certainly couldn't possibly have even imagined the massacres of innocent people and children by lunatics with high powered, rapid fire weapons. Obviously, they didn't foresee heavily armed people massacring innocents, including children in their schools. So, what could they have been thinking in instituting the second amendment; the right to bear arms?

In an age of flintlock muskets and pistols and with the Revolutionary war against the British fresh in their minds, the founding fathers wanted to be easily able to establish militia groups. That was most likely their immediate objective. Perhaps a longer-term objective was to enable an armed citizenry to resist any attempts at the establishment of a dictatorship.

We currently see quite a few dictatorships (e.g. the People's Republic of China) in the world, and many quasi dictatorships such as those of the Russian Federation, and Turkey. However, given the overarching power of most modern nations and their highly armed military forces the chances of an armed citizenry successfully resisting rotten governments are virtually zero. Military coups are quite a different matter.

It is more than obvious that the U.S.A. needs to either abolish the second amendment or drastically modify it. No amount of AR-15s and other assault rifles in the hands of civilians will be able to resist the US military. As we have seen, their only function is to enable ghastly massacre after ghastly massacre. Perhaps the National Rifle Association romantically envisages armed citizens defending the freedoms of the U.S.A. The grubby reality however is the needless and tragic number of deaths attributed to gun violence.

Be afraid of the Future

(Aug 2018)

There are too many leaders and those waiting in the wings who only care about their own egos, power and wealth and are not concerned with the good of their countries or the planet as a whole. Sensible policies and positive action are mostly ignored.

Donald Trump (from Google images)

Ego and power grabbing are all consuming. This will spell disaster for humanity and many other species.

The only real solution to the Refugee Crisis

(Aug 2019)

With every increasing human floods of refugees seeking safe havens, the world is facing a logistical nightmare in addition to increased political, social and economic problems. It is simply impracticable to have multi-millions of people traversing the world in search of a safer or better life.

The solution to the refugee crisis that is rocking the world is perhaps, glaringly simple. If people can have a safe and reasonable life in their homelands, they are not going to risk the lives of their families in leaking boats in search of a future. They are not going to line up in thousands at the Mexico/USA border either.

It would be wise for the EU to ensure that Libya has a proper government, with or without any permission. Military force would be an option. Syria is a much more difficult problem because of the involvement of Putin and the Russians. Military action there is simply not a realistic possibility.

The thousands of refugees at the Mexican/USA border are predominantly from small Central American countries where drug gangs simply run amok. It would be cheaper in the long run and more reasonable for the US to use force to clean up these small countries, with or without their cooperation, than to pursue the Trump Administration's crazy anti-immigrant policies. The only long-term solution to the refugee crisis is to clean up and rebuild the countries from where the refugees are fleeing!

Why the world's economic system destroys people
(Mar 2018)

(from Google images)

Every day we are bombarded with assertions from many of the world's governments that taxes for multinational corporations and *very rich people should be lowered*. *"It's good for the economy,"* they say, "and everybody will benefit." When the costs of lowering such taxes are pointed out, the argument runs that since other countries are doing it, we must also do it to remain competitive. Donald Trump grants huge tax concessions to the wealthy and so the other countries must follow suit.

Working poor
(from Google images)

In the somewhat optimistic decades of the 1960's and 1970's, the vast majority of people wanted to raise the wages and living standards of those in third world and other poor countries. Mind you, they also believed that technology would allow shorter working hours and higher wages! Neither of those things happened. In both the third world and in the OECD countries, working hours either stayed the same or increased and wages gradually declined against the relevant cost of living. The top 2% or so of the world, in terms of wealth, massively increased their standing while everybody else went backwards.

Without a voluntary surrendering of excess wealth nothing would ever improve. The exception proves the rule. Philanthropists like Bill

Gates and Warren Buffet make a very small proportion of the mega wealthy. It is likely that the rich getting richer and the poor becoming poorer will continue until the world's entire financial system collapses.

(from Google images)

Such economic collapse would surely be accompanied by social collapse. We haven't yet even mentioned global warming, overpopulation and the aging of the population. Scary isn't it?

Beyond Good and Evil

(Jun 2014)

The essential problem of humanity is that basically we only care about ourselves and ours. What appears to be good for us, our families and our tribes we call "good." What appears to be bad for the same we label as "bad." Greed, stupidity and most of the ills that befall our world that are caused by our species come down to the simple fact that most of us are trapped in our own egos and identities. We fail to see the big picture; our individual selves are just little tiny cogs in a much bigger environment. We must think outside of this little selfish square.

Artificial Intelligence – the way forward or precursor to the doom of humanity?

(Mar 2015)

[dreamtime.com]

Don't think of the brilliant Steven Spielberg movie with all of its predictions and pathos. Scientists and engineers in the field are widely claiming that already the learning capacity of machines is equivalent to that of an insect brain. Furthermore, they are claiming that in accordance with Moore's law, (technological advance roughly doubles every 18 months or so) by 2030 the intelligence and learning capacity of A.I. will exceed that of humans. While the use of algorithms is already quite advanced within narrow ranges, it is the capacity of artificial "brains" to learn by themselves and acquire values and opinions that is both tremendously exciting and frightening.

A super intelligent machine would be useful for its ability to find plans that its programmers never imagined, to identify shortcuts that they never noticed or considered. That capability is a double-edged sword: a machine that is extraordinarily effective at achieving its goals might have unexpected negative side effects, as in the case of robotic laboratories damaging the biosphere.

There is no simple fix: a super intelligent system would need to learn detailed information about what is and isn't considered valuable, and be motivated by this knowledge, in order to safely solve even simple tasks.

[The Value Learning Problem Nate Soares

Machine Intelligence Research Institute

nate@intelligence.org]

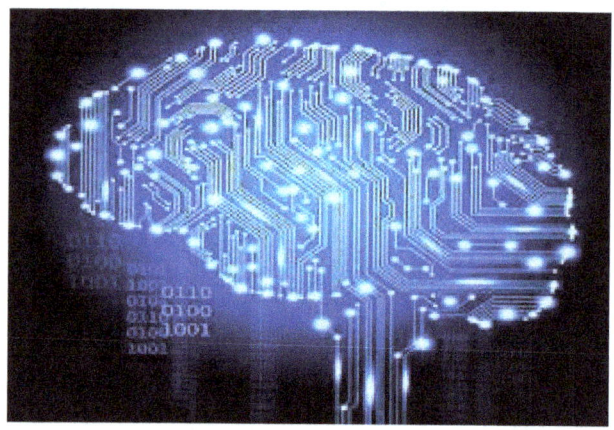

[dailysciencejournal.com]

Soares' concern doesn't even mention the possibility that such machines may acquire the value of satisfying their own issues of well-being before considering those of humanity or anything else. After all that is precisely what our species has done and why the planet's ecosystem is on the verge of collapse. Would such super intelligent examples of artificial intelligence be likely to challenge the human race as in the *Terminator* movies?

Given the advantages and risks to ourselves of continued development in this sphere should we continue with it? That is somewhat of a hypothetical question since, throughout history, humanity has never erred on the side of caution. If something can be done, it surely will. The development of artificial intelligence will continue regardless of cost or risk. This habit of our species is unstoppable regardless of whether new discoveries will prove positive or catastrophically negative.

Adam Conner-Simons describes how results of tests that were run showed that assembly line workers actually preferred a robot boss to a human one. In all likelihood this preference is a result of the machine boss not possessing the emotions, (including favouritism and prejudice,) so often exhibited by the human variety.

[Adam Conner-Simons | CSAIL

August 21, 2014]

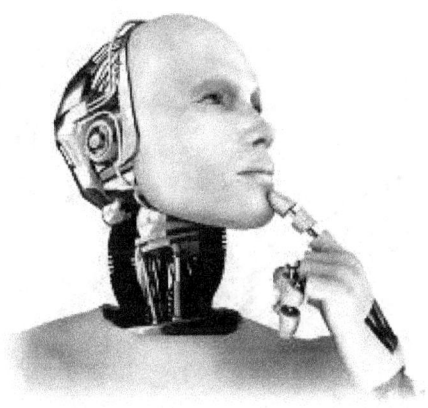

[bipb.com]

Yet the unstoppable increase in machine intelligence presumably will result in A.I. that experiences something akin to human emotions and value judgements. Will workers be happy to take orders from these more advanced bosses? In short, when the rise of machines reaches a certain but unknown point will they possess the same weaknesses and shortcomings, (in terms of emotions – including selfishness and greed) as humans but with a huge technical superiority?

To illustrate this point further think of how the human race has advanced throughout history. In prehistoric times, for example, you had two tribes warring. Each had roughly an equal number of men armed with spears. The result was probably a Mexican standoff at a very limited cost, (a few thousand dollars in terms of today's money). Now we have numbers of adversaries, (nations and groups) armed to the teeth with nuclear weapons, cyber knowledge and heaven knows what. The result is still more or less a standoff but at the cost of billions, if not trillions of dollars. Add to that the knowledge that today's weapons could spell the end of us all and we can see exactly how humanity has progressed. Technically our species has made huge strides. From a spiritual and ethical standpoint, however, we are still in the Stone Age!

When artificial intelligence takes its place in the sun will it do any better?

Adolf Hitler
(from Google images)

Hitler and Jesus were both right

(May 2013)

Jesus (and Buddha) were right in saying that you should love all things, including your enemies. On a spiritual level that is the most sensible way to approach life. Stop to sniff the flowers and love them! On a personal and individual level, that is all there is.

Yet on a biological and species level it is more than likely that Hitler was right. If one desires that humanity goes on and prospers, such ruthless policies as elimination of the disabled and weak make a great deal of sense. Post WWII the world we have inherited is worse than ever. Aging populations, ever increasing numbers of humans and finite resources are all spelling doom.

At present we have multitudes of people in nursing homes, many with dementia. In the near future; (unless humanity entirely becomes enlightened) I can't see the rich and the greedy sacrificing anything for these unproductive individuals. I suspect it will be a case of "Arbeit macht frei" (Work sets you free). You guessed correctly, that is a slogan of Nazi Germany.

I don't have to dream very hard to imagine a coming world where people who no longer work are disposed of. No, this is not a world created by Hitler. This is the world that prospered after his defeat. It is more than just for amusement, economic advancement and the occupation of time that the elderly continue to work. It probably makes them feel safer.

After all, if humanity doesn't quickly get its act together, both from an individual and species perspective, nature almost certainly will remove us, one way or the other.

Are the ever-increasing financial complexities of the contemporary world destroying your peace of mind?

Time and money are becoming increasingly intertwined and more difficult to manage.

(from Google images)

If you are over 40 you may well remember the days when most goods and services had a roughly standard price. Technology was comparatively in its infancy and life could be lived within relatively simple human equations. Work may have been arduous enough but retirement was a realistic goal with a comfortable pension or super-annuation to see you through your old age.

(from Google images)

The world has changed in a blink of an eye. People are forced to gamble with their retirement incomes by choosing safe, moderate or aggressive portfolio investments. The ordinary man is forced to make extraordinary and difficult choices. The wrong choice will condemn him or her to miserable twilight years or early extinction.

(from Google images)

Even the simplest of tasks such as shopping now involve considerable intellectual endeavour. Prices for items or services vary wildly from one outlet to the next and sensible purchasing involves extra research and time. As well as traditional stores there are now thousands of online ones. Except for the wealthy few, choices for all purchases from food to big-ticket items are matters of vital importance. The weekly grocery shop involves looking constantly for specials and only buying those. In all probability, the price of a special is what the price of the item should be in any case.

Simple financial survival in the day-to-day world is becoming an increasing headache. The countless advertisements bombarding us further damage our equilibrium. We are continually told that brand X sports drink will save us from dehydration and damage, while in truth simple tap water will do just as well for all but the most extreme of athletes and even then it is a toss-up. The very vitamins that we used to intake with a healthy balanced diet are now being marketed to us at a high price as a "must have" if we are to avoid ill-health.

Rupert Murdoch caricature
(from Google images)

The web of lies, disinformation and complexity doesn't end there. Politicians bend the truth with increasing alacrity and the mass media are ready to support their chosen ones with all sorts of distortions. The unfettered support of the Murdoch Empire for its pet causes and politicians beggars belief. To see past all this spin, which threatens our own and our children's existence, requires a considerable effort and time on our part in doing our own research. It is now no longer sufficient to read a newspaper and believe that we are basically receiving facts and truth. Now it is necessary to search countless sources, including social media, to arrive at reasonable conclusions.

(from Google images)

Life appears to be becoming more complex by the minute. Let's just hope we are all close to being geniuses and can accomplish all the tasks required of us in record time. If that is not the case something big will have to give. It will either be the excesses of capitalism or our own wellbeing if not actual survival. On every front, from intellectual to economic, the world is becoming one categorically divided into winners and losers. Mind you, if the environment goes, everyone and everything will be a bigtime loser.

Environment, Society and Economy

(Aug 2013)

As political players around the world have tried to recover from the GFC one wonders what the ultimate objectives are. Austerity seems to create as many problems as it solves; spending other people's money to spur the economy does likewise and in the meantime, we can see our environment crapping out at a rate of knots. Most politicians have valued economy, society and the environment in that exact order: the wrong order.

Using common sense, we can see that there has to be an intelligent balance between environment, social justice and economy. Protecting the environment has to come first; both for ourselves and the other creatures on the planet. If we have any pretence at all of a reasonable social order; then social justice and a sustainable, as fair as possible, society must be a priority. That leaves economy. If we mean by economy that you can't spend wealth that has not been created that is a correct assumption, (although many governments love to spend money that they hope to raise in the future from taxes on a probably impoverished generation). On the other hand, if economy means a robust capitalistic system that enables the rich to get richer, then we should simply forget about that particular parameter.

BREXIT – LIKE A BITTER, EXPENSIVE AND UNNECESSARY DIVORCE WHERE EVERYBODY LOSES

Marriage counselling would have been better for the UK and EU. A hasty divorce will hurt the children (Scotland, Northern Ireland and London). Who knows which parent (the UK or the EU) each child will live with?

(Jul 2016)

The decision to continue with the likely disastrous Brexit process on the result of the flimsiest and most careless of referendums is strange to say the least. The pound continues its slide and the future looks extremely uncertain. The current situation with the incoming PM, Theresa May, preparing to press ahead willy-nilly is analogous to a lengthy, acrimonious, expensive and unnecessary divorce.

Theresa May
(from Google images)

Sure, there are problems with quite a few of the EU arrangements. However, to refuse to deal with these within the existing structure is like a refusal to accept marriage counselling. It seems that the British government is determined to press ahead with a hasty divorce that will hurt the children, Scotland, Northern Ireland and London. The expense will be massive and both the UK and the EU will be seriously damaged as a result for little actual, positive gain.

David Cameron
(from Google images)

Outgoing PM, David Cameron, appears like a shell-shocked husband and father who has suddenly been served divorce papers from out of the blue. The shock seems to have caused him to meekly accept the catastrophe and impending disaster rather than fight against it.

It is interesting to note that the architects of this divorce, Nigel Farage, Boris Johnson and his double-crossing sidekick (analogous to greedy, self-seeking divorce lawyers), have removed themselves in one way or another from dealing with the mess.

The British parliament is the only body that can introduce Article 50 and begin the process of leaving the EU. There is no legal compulsion for them to do this. Nigel Farage (in an interview with Australian 60 Minutes) claimed that there is however, a moral one.

In view of the entire situation, just about any reasonable person would surely claim that, in light of the facts that have appeared since the Brexit vote, there is a moral imperative that they do not introduce Article 50 to a vote and pass it. Whether they decide to hold a second referendum or not, Article 50 should be left alone and considered as a virtual atomic bomb. There will be no turning back once this missile is launched and the button should NOT be pushed.

The missile was launched. However, it is still just possible that it can be recalled.

Julian Assange – champion of Freedom and Transparency

The Assange case exposes the common trumping of justice by power and politics

(Feb 2016)

In the contemporary world very few things make me at all proud of being Australian. However, the fact that Julian Assange is a country man of mine and from the state where I live, is one of those few. For years he and Wikileaks, the organisation he founded, have strived to expose gross wrongdoing and corruption on the part of governments, worldwide. Unfortunately, such wrongdoing and corruption is the norm rather than the exception. Unsurprisingly, the targets of these attacks use any and all methods to strike back.

Julian Assange
(from Google images)

The very recent UN judgement that Assange's predicament is a form of detention, unfair, unreasonable and a violation of human rights cannot but be seen as a substantive vindication of the justice of his cause. His fear of being extradited to the USA and receiving a massive judicial punishment for his whistle blowing activities, can hardly be viewed as unreasonable or unfounded. One of the Wikileaks informants, Bradley Manning, is currently serving a massively lengthy jail sentence in that country.

The fact that the United Kingdom and Sweden are currently ignoring this UN judgement is also less than surprising. Both countries (as is Australia for that matter) are heavily leveraged by the USA's power base and situation. They simply dare not challenge the government of the USA on this question as they would have too much to lose.

Additionally, I can't imagine any governments that would enjoy their secrets being exposed by Wikileaks. Corruption and abuse of power is so much the norm that it is probably the major reason that humanity is rather quickly descending into a gloomy and miserable future. The USA may be bad enough but the governments of Russia and China are probably much worse. Undoubtedly, they would be hot on Assange's trail if he had managed to expose their darkest malfeasances. If that had been the case, he may not have even been alive now.

It is becoming obvious that, around the world, ordinary honest people are becoming increasingly marginalised and finding it more difficult to simply survive. Fewer and fewer champions of any semblance of decency are to be found.

The symbol of Anonymous
(from Google images)

Organisations such as Anonymous, appear to be largely noble-minded rather than self-serving. All over the world, most politicians are commonly viewed as feeding at the trough at our expense. The few admirable ones seem to support the adage that the exception proves the rule. Of course, part of the human condition involves imperfection and inconsistency.

Politicians may sometimes act for the common good and then return to the old habits. Also, the better world leaders are often constrained by the undesirable powers behind them. It may well be the case that personally, Barrack Obama, would like to publicly abandon any pursuit of Assange. However, this is simply not possible. Obama hasn't thus far safeguarded his improvements to the US health system and has made almost no headway in gun control. Mind you, fear of governments and politicians has probably contributed to the resistance about changes to the Second Amendment.

Donald Trump
(from Google images)

Despite his outrageous and populist statements Donald Trump has done very well so far in the presidential race. In all likelihood this success comes down to two facts. Firstly, he is NOT a politician (so far). Secondly, he is using his own money to fund his campaign.

In a non-politically correct world Julian Assange might be accused of having attractive females representing him as legal counsel.

Jennifer Robinson, Julian Assange's lawyer
(from Google images)

Since this is a politically correct word, except in so far as justice and honesty are concerned, Jennifer Robinson's looks are entirely irrelevant to the whole Assange question. Likewise, any other female spokespersons who act on his behalf cannot be considered on any other grounds than their integrity and ability.

In all probability the old allegations of sexual misconduct originating from the Swedish Prosecutor's office are anything but fair and reasonable. Increasingly, the entire Assange case looks like a case of a corrupt and powerful Goliath attempting to squash a little 'David'.

The whole Assange case and its ramifications for World powers exposes the most alarming of situations. Although terrorist organisations, such as ISIS, ISIL, Daish, Islamic State or whatever they call themselves, are quite apparently grossly barbaric and driven by a lunatic ideology, they have one thing going for them.

The blindingly obvious corruption of the majority of governments around the world, and particularly over the Middle East, fuels support for any entity that is standing and fighting these governments. Under current circumstances, any organisation challenging the world status quo would receive wide support amongst the impressionable young particularly. Given ISIS's skilful use of social media as a way of sidestepping the world's power base their hitherto success in attracting foreign fighters is hardly surprising.

Islamic State fighters
(from Google images)

Bombs and warfare alone will not put Syria, Libya, Iraq and much of the world back in order. To regain public support and belief; the world powers must reform their own houses first. Chasing Julian Assange and other whistle blowers to the ends of the earth is hardly the way to do this!

Populism, short-sightedness and the height of Folly

As the challenges facing humanity grow more and more complex and difficult to overcome it is natural that people look with critical eyes on the ruling establishments and desire a quick fix. However, quick "fixes" generally only exacerbate underlying problems rather than providing a real solution. With the proliferation of possible news sources, it is becoming increasingly difficult to know what to believe.

(Feb 2017)

Theresa May
(from Google images)

Taking advantage of democracy's essential weakness (the lowest common denominator factor) populist movements and leaders have sprung into action around the globe. Fear of immigrants had much to do with the foolish Brexit vote. Despite the fact that most of the UK's voters now have a much clearer idea of what the real costs of Brexit will be, Theresa May and her government seem determined to carry on with this folly rather than offering the people a second referendum. The likely outcome will be the breakup of the UK itself in addition to a very large economic burden.

There is no denying that the EU needs a significant amount of reform. It expanded too fast admitting several countries whose economies were too low compared with the UK, France, Germany and Italy. This, coupled with the fact that many Europeans can speak English while relatively few British people can speak a European language, means that the UK receives a net immigration from the EU. Despite this only genuine complaint that the Brexiteers might have, the cost to the UK and to Europe as a whole of Brexit and a weakened EU is just far too high.

Donald Trump
(from Google images)

The election of Donald Trump to the presidency of the USA is another example of voters being so desperate for change that they forget that a disastrous change is much worse than no change at all. With an unpredictable loose cannon in the White House, the USA and the world must surely experience increasing levels of anxiety.

Marine Le Pen
(france24.com)

The third apex of the triangle hasn't happened yet. If far right leaders, such as Marine Le Pen succeed in their presidential bids in upcoming European elections the collapse of the European Union would seem all but a certainty. The loss of Britain is a huge blow for the EU but the additional loss of France would be fatal. The collapse of the EU would be disastrous for Europe and the world. The outbreak of more armed conflict in the region would be all but certain.

With Putin's Russia prepared to assert itself at all costs and China's determination to steal sovereignty of much of the South China Sea the world is becoming an increasingly dangerous place. It is no wonder the Doomsday clock was reset at two and a half minutes to midnight after the inauguration of Donald Trump.

We haven't even considered yet that global warming and climate change is increasing all the time and has probably already reached tipping point and that the looney dictator of North Korea, Kim Jong Un is getting ever closer to having nuclear ICBMs. As the main suspect in the recent murder of his estranged half-brother, Kim Jong Un apparently will stop at nothing to maintain his grip on power. While the war in Syria drags on and millions of innocents suffer, the power brokers in the world seem much more concerned with their own well-being than with any ethics, altruism or even common sense.

Kim Jong Un leader of North Korea
(from Google images)

We are facing desperate times. Any more short-sighted populist quick fixes are likely to throw us all over the edge.

The Evil Triangle of World Power

(Apr 2018)

Donald Trump

Vladimir Putin

Xi JinpIng

(all above photographs from Google images)

Donald Trump, to put it nicely, appears to be erratic, unable to formulate any reasonable and consistent policy and seems to lack the moral compass and integrity required for a U.S. president. His election campaign was centred round the phrase, "Make America great again." It is more than unlikely that he will even vaguely succeed in this quest. Most of the good news about the U.S. economy is a result of the efforts of his predecessor, Barack Obama.

Vladimir Putin, the president of Russia, has the aim of basically restoring the Soviet Union to its former powerful position and is prepared to invade countries (the Ukraine and Crimea) and overlook or contribute to the murder of innocents, including children (his support of Assad's regime in Syria) in pursuit of this goal. He is pursuing any means available, including cyber warfare, in pursuit of his aim. He even had the temerity to tell Russians to prepare for possible nuclear attack. His mojo might as well be called, "Make Russia great again" and he is effectively conducting a semi-clandestine war against the West.

Xi Jinping, China's president for life, wants to make the "reunification" of China his legacy. (One must remember that the original inhabitants of Taiwan were not Chinese, and that it is only in the last three centuries that large numbers of Chinese people inhabited that island. Taiwan is not, and was not, an integral part of China.) He has said that China is prepared to use force to take Taiwan.

He also desires to extend Chinese power as far into the Pacific as he possibly can. You might as well say that he wishes to make China great, or greater again and probably aims to make it the world's number one super power. Again, questions of morality or legality are not even considered. Here we have another dangerous maniac in full flight.

These three presidents, Trump, Putin and Xi, are much more likely to cause a catastrophic nuclear war than achieve their aims. None of them knows how to be sensible, reasonable and back down when necessary. We have every reason to be scared, and much more so than in 1962.

China's uncompromising plan to take over much of the world

(Dec 2018)

Xi Jinping President (or more correctly, Chairman) of China
(slate.com)

China, under President for life, Xi Jinping, has set a course to "conquer" as much of the world as possible; covertly (with bribery and bullying "loans" to small and vulnerable nations), and overtly such as the takeover of much of the South China Sea and the simple denial of historical fact as is the case concerning Taiwan.

The really terrifying aspect of China's march is an apparent total lack of a moral compass. The current trial of China's social credit system is "1984" stuff. Everyone is photographed and a file kept on the entire population. Those who are good Party members etc. can travel wherever they like and can afford to. Others who might buy too much liquor or criticize the government, suddenly find themselves unable to even travel to the next town. They are stopped from boarding trains or buses etc.

The recent admission of genetic alteration of human embryos by a Chinese scientist could be even scarier. It is not a huge stretch to see a future where human embryos are altered to create model citizens and die-hard supporters of the Chinese government.

We should be afraid, very afraid.

Theresa May's Brexit obsession is a recipe for disaster

(Dec 2018)

Theresa May
(from Google images)

Despite a number of prominent leaders in the UK, including two former PMs stating that a second Brexit referendum is the only sensible thing to do, Mrs. May erroneously thinks that another referendum would further divide the nation. Perhaps her aim is simply to go down in history in a big way. The nation is already bitterly divided and headed downhill fast. A second referendum with all the options on the table is the only way to move forward.

Carrying on with her chosen course is only likely to divide the nation further. Scotland and Northern Ireland will demand independence referendums, (the second for Scotland and the first for Northern Ireland) and the breakup of the UK is a likely result. If this is not further dividing the UK then what is?

The UK and Europe at the Crossroads

(Mar 2017)

Recent weeks have been momentous in the unfolding of the fate of Western Europe and the Western world generally. Scotland is now clamouring for a second independence referendum. As far as Scotland is concerned the Brexit folly was the last straw. Nicola Sturgeon, Scotland's First Minister, is leading a determined push for another independence referendum and soon.

Nicola Sturgeon
(from Google images)

Theresa May's insistence that such a referendum can only be granted by Westminster is hardly likely to placate the Scots.

British PM Theresa May
(from Google images)

A very real possibility of the breakup of the UK is now presenting itself. It would be much simpler and more sensible to have a second

Brexit referendum. Such a referendum could simply be the conduct of another vote, without any campaigning since most of the British public now have a fair idea of what Brexit would entail, including many undesirable consequences that they hadn't even considered at the time of the referendum last June. If Theresa May's government needs an excuse to hold a second referendum it needn't look very far.

Further evidence that Putin's Russia may have not only interfered in the US's presidential election but may have been involved in the financing of Donald Trump's business interests, (when Wall Street wouldn't touch him) has presented itself.

Donald Trump
(whitehouse.gov)

Vladimir Putin
(businessinsider.com)

Some British MPs have claimed that Putin's Russia may have interfered in the Brexit campaign. Even the possibility of this would be a perfectly reasonable excuse for holding a second Brexit referendum vote.

It is quite clear that Putin has been conducting a clandestine campaign to destabilise Western Europe and the EU as part of his aim to make Russia a great power again. "Make Russia great again" has a familiar ring doesn't it? His bloody and bloody-minded support of Assad has cost the lives of countless innocents and created the greatest refugee crisis since WW II. To be accurate the Soviet Union (and Russia) had a lot to do with that refugee crisis too.

Assad President of Syria
(from Google images)

Putin obviously knew that his support of Assad's regime would prolong that hideous civil war and send millions of refugees in the direction of Western Europe and the EU.

The Netherlands' very recent election has resulted in the return of the current Dutch PM. In resisting populist and far right politics, have the Dutch people shown themselves to be fundamentally more intelligent and thoughtful than the British and the Americans, or is it a case of the Dutch having seen the unfortunate results of the Brexit debacle and the election of Donald Trump?

Although under the American political system it would be very difficult to dislodge Donald Trump now, (impeachment seems a very unlikely possibility) and you can just forget about the removal of Putin in Russia, it is very simple for Britain to conduct a second Brexit referendum vote. It would seem that Theresa May wants to rush through the Brexit folly and trigger article 50 as a sign of her power. Perhaps she would also like to go down in history as the person who did the most to destroy the UK and hugely damage Western Europe.

Marine Le Pen (leader of France's National Front)
(from Google images)

If the French, in their coming presidential election, can resist the fallacious populist appeal of the far right, then perhaps Europe has a chance. However, if they elect Marie Le Pen and France leaves the EU, the European Union will be finished and Western Europe will be massively damaged and in a worse situation than it was prior to the Second World War.

The person with the greatest opportunity to stop this disastrous slide is Theresa May. If the British government decides to hold a second vote on Brexit before the French elections are held, a clear signal will have been sent that the West will resist the attempts of Putin to bring it to its knees. Hope in a reasonable future could then return.

Vladimir Putin's War on the West

Vladimir Putin
(from en.wikipedia.com)

(Dec 2018)

A person may wonder why the Russian Federation, under Putin's leadership, would not only support but actively assist Assad's murderous Syrian regime in its disgustingly vile and brutal attacks on children and other civilians under the guise of attacking rebels/terrorists. It is becoming increasingly obvious to anyone with a modicum of intelligence that Mr. Putin will stop at nothing in his cherished attempt to recreate a Russian (Soviet style) empire in Europe. Evidence for this includes the annexation of the Crimea and support for rebels attacking the forces of the Ukraine.

His, all but absolutely proven, interference in the US presidential election and the Brexit referendum are additional evidence that he desires nothing short of a massive weakening of Europe, starting with the EU, and of the United States. Who can tell what his ambitions will result in after a sufficient weakening of the West?

It is almost certain that he will position Russia as close as possible to China, (remember, the Chinese president has more dictatorial power than any of his predecessors) and do all he can to promote subtle forms of conflict between the USA and Chinese. This would be largely economic, (both Russia and China are hoarding gold and trying to reduce any dependence on the US dollar) but may well include promoting some degree of military confrontation. I am not suggesting, however, that Putin wants to start any kind of nuclear war.

Returning to the horrors occurring in Syria and the myriad images of severely injured children on our TVs, we again ask ourselves why does Putin support this horror? Only a day or so ago the Russian ambassador to the UN vetoed a proposal to establish a ceasefire in that heavily bombarded rebel enclave near Damascus. The answer, although horrifying, is relatively simple. The lives of all those children and others mean nothing to Putin compared with his aim of massively weakening the West.

Without Russia's intervention in Syria it is probable that the civil war in Syria would be largely over by now. Putin wants to keep it going so that the flow of refugees to the West is ever increasing. This flood of refugees certainly weakens the strength and economies of Western Europe, (regardless of cultural questions such as the possible Islamisation of those countries). When you think about it, without the flood of refugees into Europe the British Brexit referendum is likely to have gone the other way.

The "Leave" campaign dishonestly distributed leaflets showing unnamed maps of Syria and Iraq. This fear of a refugee horde undoubtedly influenced many British voters to support the Brexit idea. It is becoming increasingly clear how much of a disaster, both for the UK and the EU, Brexit will be. Only today the President of the EU made a public statement that Theresa May is living in a fantasy land as regards her wish list for Brexit.

One thing is certain: Vladimir Putin will be smiling. Many historians argue that both Stalin and Mao were even worse than Hitler was, as regards crimes against humanity and the number of deaths of innocents that they caused. Perhaps in the future Vladimir Putin will be added to that vile list.

What the rise of China, Putin's Russia, America's Donald Trump and Brexit mean for Freedom

Xi Jinping
(news.yahoo.com)

As if the looming disasters of climate change and overpopulation aren't enough, we now face a huge challenge to our very notion of freedom. Although Xi Jinping's China could hardly be called a socialist or communist society, it has a massive ideological agenda built around authoritarian power. This China could best be described as a state-run capitalist oligarchy with loads of attendant corruption.

Recent history is likely to provoke ample alarm. From building military fortifications on an artificial island in the South China Sea to unilaterally claiming the Spratleys, China has ignored the other claimants to those regions and forged ahead in its quest to become the world's greatest military and economic power, leaving any notions of freedom and human rights dead in its wake.

Any vague notion of liberty for the billion odd inhabitants in that country was quickly dispelled with the advent of the new social credit system, whereby the smallest transgressions against the state ideal can result in a person being unable to leave his or her home town.

The "One Belt One Road" program has amounted to China making loans to poor countries in the Pacific and Africa and, when those nations are unable to repay, they become vassals of China. It doesn't take a genius to see where all this is going. If you didn't like the USA's behaviour when it dominated the planet you "ain't seen nothin' yet" as China's ascendancy rises. Xi Jinping's installation as leader for life (read absolute dictator) is the icing on the cake.

Bob Hawke
(from Google images)

Kevin Rudd
(from Google images)

Australia is caught in an ungodly position. Its defence strategy depends heavily on the USA but its main trading partner is China. The chair of parliament's powerful Security and Intelligence Committee, Andrew Hastie warned Australia against underestimating China and compared its rise to that of Nazi Germany and Stalin's Soviet Union. Unsurprisingly, this didn't go down well with China.

How did this unfortunate position happen to Australia? It is fair to blame the Australian Labor Party. Bob Hawke began Australia's dependence on China and Kevin Rudd increased it. Under their policies Australia has experienced a huge increase in immigration from mainland China. The big problem here lies in the fact that many of these people consider that their first loyalty is to China. Xi Jinping has also stated that such Australian citizens owe such first loyalty to China.

Putin and Xi
(chinadaily.com)

China's strategic alliance with Putin's Russia, (another authoritarian state, although it denies it) presents major challenges to the Western countries which value freedom. Putin's Russia is another nation hell bent on increasing its power at all costs. Its track record includes the annexation of Crimea, starting a war in the Ukraine, and direct complicity in countless civilian deaths, including children, in Syria. It is safe to say that without Putin's intervention the war in Syria would have finished years ago. Strangely enough Putin is popular with the majority of Russians. Of course, like the Chinese, they probably don't have all that much access to unfiltered or uncensored information.

The China-Russia duo is a massive assault on the West and its notion of freedom. This brings us to the Brexit debacle. Only by remaining united under the EU can Western Europe withstand the political and possibly military assault from the East. It has been established that Russia interfered in both the Brexit referendum and the U.S. presidential election, which resulted in the installation of Donald Trump.

The Cambridge Analytica saga demonstrated how cunning use of personal information can achieve political ends. It is true that Trump is challenging China's unfair trade practices. However, he is doing it in the most foolish of ways. Instead of joining forces with the EU he insisted on America going it alone. He even imposed tariffs on steel from the EU along with goods from China. Trump seems to love the idea of Brexit. Along with fellow narcissist and ego maniac Boris Johnson, the new British PM, Trump projects an enormous optimism in the face of an ever-increasing danger.

Donald Trump narcissist
(from Google images)

Boris Johnson fellow narcissist
(from Google images)

Both of these men downplayed the seriousness of the Covid-19 pandemic but Johnson changed his mind after nearly dying from the disease. (July 2020)

Once Britain leaves the EU, Trump has planned a new trade deal between Britain and the USA. This trade deal would very likely involve a massive weakening of Britain's National Health system and make health care as unaffordable for many as it is in the U.S. Donald Trump is obviously intending to challenge both Britain and the EU economically.

Divide and conquer. Xi Jinping and Putin must be laughing themselves sick. It is small wonder that the USA hates Julian Assange and Wikileaks. The only reason that China and Russia aren't after him as well lies in the fact that he wasn't able to get his hands on any of their dirty secrets. Whistle-blowers are a rarity in those two authoritarian states as the penalties are so extreme that fear prevails.

The almost total loss of privacy doesn't just exist in China and Russia. Social media invasions, along with almost universal camera and detection systems, are on the rise in the West. Under the guise of security, states around the world are increasing their control over their citizens. The use of algorithms doesn't just mean targeted ads. It is also likely to mean extremely accurate predictors of human behaviour.

It would appear that the only thing George Orwell got wrong was the date!

(from Google images)

Islamist Jihad, Freedom, Refugees and Human Rights

(Mar 2015)

Capitalism, delusional masses and endless war

Isis fighters
(cfr.org)

(Mar 2015)

Terrorism and Islamic jihad are on the increase almost everywhere, from the nightly news to neighbourhoods perhaps only a few miles away. The burning and oft discussed question is, "How do we end this delusional violence while protecting the freedoms and human rights of all?" Western folk often used to condemn teenage rebellion and the fondness of the young for sex, drugs and rock n' roll. This social phenomenon seems somewhat mild compared with its Islamic equivalent. In order to have a realistic chance of ending this sickening and savage violence, humanity needs to understand the causes in all their complexity and have the courage to act.

Wars fought in the name of religion are the height of stupidity and ignorance. However, such wars often have much deeper causes and issues beneath the surface.

Beliefs in themselves

It is absurd to try to coerce others as to their beliefs. People can believe what they like and nobody can stop them from this in any case. Muslims, and others, have a perfect right to believe whatever they will. Such beliefs may be illogical, self-delimiting and crazy but the person holding them can continue to do so regardless, until such time as Orwell's thought police become a reality. In fact, faced with a jihadi sword, many a potential victim must have pretended to convert to the particular enforced version of Islam. Certainly, overt actions such as religious observances and rituals can be monitored but a person's actual set of beliefs remains immune. Legislation or force cannot change a person's beliefs. Only education and knowledge can effectively impact on humanity's belief systems.

Actions and the Rights of Others

(from Google images)

It would seem inherently reasonable that people can pray and perform rituals however they wish, as long as their practices do not harm or interfere with the rights and freedoms of others. Likewise, they should be able to keep elements of their native cultures, as long as that culture does not interfere with the rights of others or with the cultural traditions of the lands in which they live.

In the case of Islamic folk who reside in the West, this should and must mean that the **practice** of their religion does not interfere with the right of free speech; including the right to criticise or satirise anything, or with long established traditions such as Christmas. Most people in Western countries are able to not only tolerate but also have a laugh at religious jokes that appear amusing. It is sad that so many followers of Islam seem to have lost their sense of humour.

(from Google images)

The Rights of Refugees

(from Google images)

In the wake of anti-Islamic sentiment that has followed terrorist attacks and the pursuit of jihad, western nations have experienced public demonstrations of opposition, and often downright hostility, to the arrival of refugees from Muslim lands. Surely, we don't want to harden our hearts against those, particularly children, who through no fault of their own are in desperate need. Genuine refugees, who appreciate the kindness of their host nations and are prepared to co-operate with the cultures and laws of their new homes, should be welcomed and assisted.

Unsurprisingly, a problem is always at the ready to spring up! In this case it appears in the guise of significant numbers of refugees who are unwilling to co-operate with the cultures, practices and laws of their host nations. These individuals cannot simply be dismissed as a few jihadis who pretended to be refugees and arrived in western countries as sleepers, ready to strike at any time. The numbers of "home grown" terrorists in western nations and jihadis who travel to the Middle East to join ISIS are too great to be explained in such a way.

Islamic demonstrator
(from Google images)

A more rational explanation is that there are large enough numbers of refugees who flee countries where war, Islamic jihad and terrorism are rife, find homes in the west, and then seek to introduce, if not impose, the very elements of their original culture and interpretation of Islam that were the major causes of the destruction of their original countries in the first place. In many cases it is the children of these particular immigrants who, despite being born and raised in the west, are now active proponents of radical Islam and jihad.

I take pains to emphasise that these particular immigrants, although a sizeable enough number, are still a small minority of refugees. These uncompromising jihadi types who bite the very hand that feeds them can be compared to a spreading cancer. It is these individuals and their practice of Islam that need to be stamped out and quickly. The grateful refugees should still be welcome. It is beyond obvious that refugee screening procedures should be more thorough than they have been in the past. Nevertheless, we have still to examine the underlying causes of all this wanton violence and terror!

Capitalism, War and the Arab Spring

(from Google images)

It is no accident that the Arab Spring occurred before the rise of ISIS and the rapid increase in jihadi terrorism. For decades the despots in many of the Arab nations have stolen their populaces blind. Likewise, western nations have profited from the poverty of those populations while propping up corrupt and despotic regimes for the west's own perceived geo-political interests. The failure of the Arab Spring to improve the ordinary people's lives fuelled just about every kind of extremist violence imaginable. With nowhere to turn it is unsurprising that unemployed and dispossessed youths flocked to extremist calls.

History tells us that it is economics more than actual notions of freedom that spur underclasses into action. Modern day China is a case in point. Despite a lack of freedom there the rulers have managed to keep a lid on discontent by substantially increasing living standards (economically at any rate) for large numbers of the population.

The young people of the Middle East have seen any vestiges of an opportunity for a decent life slip away or stolen from them. Despite the almost unimaginable horror and brutality of ISIS and their jihadi cohorts, they appear relatively free from the stain of corruption that hangs over the traditional rulers and the western powers. Hence it is small wonder that thousands flock to what they see (probably unconsciously) as their last hope. Add to that the recipe of excitement and "idealism" and the mix is a very potent one. Many youngsters have joined ISIS to the horror of their own parents.

War and Capitalism

(from Google images)

Those of us who have read George Orwell's novel, "1984," can probably see the ghastly parallel between his three super nations, constantly at war with each other, along with the occasional change in alliance structure, and our modern world. The mega rich and their greed have their interests served by perpetual conflict and war as these assist the capitalist model nicely.

After all, those who decide on having wars don't actually fight in them. It is ordinary folk who fight and die for the wealth and power of others. Freedom and human rights are never served by wars, (in the long run at least) as nothing ever really changes for the better. Different groups of powerful mega rich keep the game running as our world society and environment deteriorate in a spiral that is rapidly running out of control.

Without fundamental reform of human society and capitalism any military victory over Islamic jihadism or any other form of ultra violence will be shortlived. There will always be more greedy and powerful individuals and more expressions of radical terror!

Self empowerment of the People

Anonymous hacker group
(from Google images)

If there is any solution at all to the woes that are bringing the human species down at an exponential rate it probably lies in the anarchist dictum; "People, do not replace overthrown rulers with others that will do the same, but rule yourselves from the ground up!" [my own statement]

Recep Tayyip Erdoğan

(Mar 2019)

The murder of 50 innocent people, and the injuring of many more by a nameless Australian man at two mosques in Christchurch has brought out the best and worst in humanity. The New Zealand Prime Minister, Jacinda Ardern, and the emergency services in Christchurch all performed magnificently showing their empathy and genuine humanity. This is quite apart from their efficiency in minimising the effects of this horrible tragedy as much as possible. .

Recep Tayyip Erdoğan (abc.net.au)

Alas. the same cannot be said for the President of Turkey. Erdoğan couldn't resist making stupid inflammatory comments to bolster up support from his radical Islamist base before upcoming elections. His remarks about sending home people with anti-islamist attitudes in coffins, particularly Australians, if they visited Turkey are of the same ilk as the views of the nameless assassin of those innocent people in the mosques. What does this turkey (the president not the country) want? More violence and more terrorism?

To add ignorance and absurdity to his statements he said that the Gallipoli campaign of 1915 was an attack by the Anzacs against Islam. How ludicrous! The attack on Turkey was an attempted backdoor strike against Germany, a Christian country that was allied with Turkey in the Great War. Religion had nothing whatsoever to do with it.

The great Ataturk, the founder of modern Turkey, took great care to make Turkey a secular state and quickly forgave the Anzacs for their attack. After that Australia, New Zealand and Turkey became great friends. The lunatic current president of Turkey, by his extremist promotion of Islam has not only prevented his country from joining the EU but is also endangering its membership of NATO.

This is not to even mention his strident steps towards creating a dictatorship; jailing his critics at the slightest pretext. No wonder the Turkish military attempted a coup. How else could they protect the legacy of Ataturk? It is a shame that the coup didn't succeed! Let's just hope that the people of Turkey will quickly wake up and see this man for what he is and how he is attempting to destroy a previously happy and successful nation!

Were Nazi Economics the Real Cause of WW II?

(Mar 2015)

Alred Rosenberg
(from Google images)

In his "Myth of the Twentieth Century", Alfred Rosenberg stated the essence of Nazi economics. He declared that capital was nothing more than the value of stored labor. In short, the Nazis saw capital as the savings, put away for the future, of the fruits of labour, honestly earned.

They did not approve of the capitalistic system of the present world, where the rich get richer (without work) and the poor get poorer (with more and more work). Despite the various crimes of the Third Reich their economic policy was second to none. They achieved a balance between capital and labor that not only made sense but was also fair. Some elements of the Nazi party, including the Strasser brothers, wanted to outright ban any unearned income, whatsoever, apart from pensions.

Despite being reduced to an economic ruin after WW I, the Treaty of Versailles and the Great Depression, Hitler's Germany performed an economic miracle in less than five years. It was the first country in the world to fully emerge from the depression. Economically, it was the envy of most of the world. The world's bankers (both Jewish and non-Jewish) were not as pleased by Germany's brilliant progress as it threatened their world of usury and huge, easy profits. If other countries followed in the steps of Germany the banking behemoth would lose much of its ill-gotten wealth and power.

The halls of gross capitalism may well have been felled forever. Apart from Hitler's words in Mein Kampf and those of Rosenberg, there are a number of sources that suggest that a formidable banking and economic group did their best not only to keep WW I going and assist the demise of the Kaiser's Germany but also to bring about WW II. This group of virtual illuminati wanted at all costs to keep the world's dollar and borrowing systems going and were behind a worldwide Jewish boycott of Germany's trade goods early on in the Third Reich.

[Adolph Hitler, The Greatest Story Never Told - https://www.youtube.com/results?search_query=adolf+hitler+the+greatest+story+never+told+part+1] Although some sections of this 27-part documentary are not very convincing, others make a profound statement and refer to facts that are quite verifiable. This is particularly the case with its assertion that Nazi Germany's economic miracle may well have been a prime cause of WW II.

In terms of economic fairness and consideration for the environment, the defeat of the Nazis has seen no improvement for mankind and the other creatures who inhabit this planet. The GFC of 2008 was a product of the same global economic powers that the National Socialists railed against all those years ago. The greed and shortsightedness of the mega wealthy and powerful has not only caused misery for billions but is also now threatening the very fabric and survival of our world.

The Brexit Debacle

(Aug 2019)

The ludicrous situation of Brexit threating to destroy the very existence of the UK begs one very significant question: how was it that the 2016 referendum was run in such a careless way? For such a major constitutional change, surely it should have been a minimum requirement that, apart from a simple majority, there should have also been the requirement that a majority of all four countries (England, Scotland, Northern Ireland and Wales that make up the UK) agreed to leave. Generally, for such constitutional changes a 66% majority is required.

Former PM
(from Google images)

Boris Johnson, new PM
(from Google images)

Yet the diehard Brexiteers ignorant of the consequences, are taking to the streets demanding that their votes, be enshrined as the cornerstone of democracy. Common-sense demands that a second referendum be held, now that the UK populace has some idea of what is involved and the costs.

Now that Boris Johnson is the Prime Minister of the UK, the situation resulting from that flawed referendum has become even worse, as Johnson is advocating an exit from the European Union by the end of October 2019 at any price, including a no-deal Brexit which is likely to see chaos and renewed violence in Northern Ireland.

Leaders the World would be better off without

There are a considerable number of world leaders whose influence and action are predominantly negative in the struggle to achieve a happy, just and cohesive world. Here, we look at just some of the more remarkable and prominent ones amongst them. Some are downright criminals of the worst order with innocent blood on their hands. Others are corrupt and/or incompetent and yet others have short-sighted attitudes and huge egos which cause them to damage their countries and the wider world around them.

They are not listed in any particular order. While some are indeed horrendous, they lead not-so-powerful countries and their negative effects are limited largely to their own populations. Others, while not being in the same moral league, head much more powerful nations and therefore have a greater effect at large.

1. ***Kim Jong Un of North Korea***

Kim Jong Un
(guardian.com)

Kim Jong Un stands accused of many crimes and executions and has zealously developed North Korea's nuclear weapons and missile technology; undermining the stability of the region and making countries further afield nervous. Despite having the benefit of an education in Europe, he seems to be somewhat paranoid and boasts a love of absolute power, unhindered by ethical qualms.

2. ***Bashir Al Assad of Syria***

Al Assad
(from Google images)

Assad has led a murderous war against his own people that has killed hundreds of thousands of civilians, including many children, apparently without giving it any more thought than if he was just squashing flies. Right at the beginning of the demonstrations against his rule during the Arab spring, he could have simply resigned with all of his wealth intact. It was once reported that his own mother suggested he do this. Yet he was determined to remain President of Syria no matter what the cost in innocent lives.

3. *Vladimir Putin of the Russian Federation*

Vladimir Putin
(en.wikipedia.com)

Putin has ruled Russia for two decades and has managed to stifle what democracy it had when he came to power. It is obvious that he wants Russia to be the power that it once was in the glory days of the Soviet Union and is none too fussy about what means he uses to achieve that end. He apparently is doing all he can to weaken Western Europe and the United States. It seems that he did indeed attempt to influence the outcome of the U.S. presidential election last year. Surprisingly perhaps, Putin is popular with the majority of Russians and also with the Russian Orthodox Church.

The church likes his conservative stand against gay rights and the population perhaps fall for the nationalist drivel that so many of the world's people do. Apart from standing accused of having masterminded several state-sponsored murders, Putin's support of Assad's murderous regime is undoubtedly a crime against humanity. Without Putin's support the war in Syria may well have ended a couple of years ago and the dreaded ISIS may never have come into existence.

4. *Donald Trump of the United States*

Donald Trump
(forbes.com)

Regardless of whether Trump colluded with the Russians during the election campaign or not, it is becoming increasingly apparent that he simply does not have the ability to effectively govern the world's most powerful nation. A man with a huge ego and a belief in simple solutions to complex problems is simply not up to the task. Nearly six months into his presidency he seems to be still in campaign mode. His simple "solutions" often appeal to the most selfish and unreasonable side of human nature, marginalising minorities in the process. A person who is addicted to Twitter, especially one in his position, could be fairly described as a twit.

5. Nicolas Maduro of Venezuela

Nicolas Maduro
(from Google images)

Nicolas Maduro has done little if anything to fight corruption in his country and has so mismanaged it that it is facing economic ruin, social collapse and civil strife. Certainly, the falling oil price has exacerbated the economy's position but there has been no plan to develop other sources of foreign revenue and no effective measures to deal with the situation. He is clinging to power regardless of popular dissent. The recent helicopter attack on a government building has been widely reported as being possibly staged so he can further clamp down on the country's freedoms and ensure a virtual dictatorship.

6. Xi Jinping President (for Life) of China

Xi Jinping
(cnbc.com)

Apart from the fact that he apparently can't speak much English, which is disgraceful for the leader of a world power, Xi Jinping, the president of China appears not to care a fig about human rights and is set on flexing China's muscle. Like most of the other members of China's oligarchy he is more likely corrupt than not. Power seems to motivate him much more than any sense of justice or compassion. If the eyes are the window to the soul, he looks in bad shape.

He must be held largely responsible for the disgraceful treatment of dissidents in China. He also lacks a sense of humour, banning Winnie the Pooh in the nation after associations were made between himself and that famous cartoon character. If Winnie the Pooh, on any level, were to be compared with Xi Jinping, Winnie the Pooh should feel insulted.

7. Recep Tayyip Erdogan President of Turkey

Recep Tayyip Erdogan
(en.wikipedia.org)

Another destroyer of any semblance of democracy is the president of Turkey. He is a populist who makes Donald Trump look mild and harmless in comparison. His mission appears to be the destruction of the secular state established long ago by the great Ataturk and the creation of an Islamic state.

Ataturk's wisdom saved Turkey from the excesses and dramas of radical Islam and now Erdogan wants to destroy this. He has used the excuse of the failed coup to jail many thousands of people, and dismiss from their jobs hundreds of thousands more and markedly increase his own power through a narrow referendum result. At the end of the day many people are probably sorry that the coup wasn't successful.

8. *Rodrigo Duterte President of the Philippines*

Rodrigo Duterte
(from Google images)

Duterte came to power as his tough stance on the war on drugs appealed to many voters. There is no denying that the Philippines has had a serious drug problem for many years. Amongst the worst of those drugs is Meth Amphetamine or Crystal Meth, known in the West as "Ice" but in the Philippines as "Shabu." This drug reached prominence in the Philippines more than 20 years before it grabbed headlines in Western countries.

Many of these addicts in the Philippines have been responsible for countless murders, in addition to robberies and other crimes. "Addis-addis," as they are called in the local language, have provoked fear and loathing across the nation. The police already knew how to deal with the worst of them. Multiple murderers, who terrified potential witnesses so much that none would testify against them, would often be found dead in a ditch somewhere. This extra-judicial removal of the most terrifying of criminals is known in the Philippines as "Salvage." Although this "Salvage" may offend Westerners' sense of legal niceties, in this country it has been actually necessary quite often.

Yet Duterte has actively promoted the extra judicial killing of many thousands of people, including those who were simply selling a little marijuana. Along with such relatively harmless folk it would seem that his war on drugs has included the elimination of political rivals without any convincing proof at all. He has even expelled foreign missionaries who dared to criticise him.

9. *Hun Sen President of Cambodia*

Hun Sen
(from Google images)

The president of Cambodia is another leader who boasts a love affair with power. Despite having the benefit of an education in Australia he hasn't adopted any principles of democracy or social justice. He rules his country with an iron fist and it is most unlikely he will ever be removed by popular will.

10. Boris Johnson new Prime Minister of the UK

Boris Johnson
(from Google images)

Boris Johnson is notoriously known for his insistence on any form of Brexit, including a no-deal one, by the end of October 2019.

This man, who was once a colourful and unconventional major of London, has quite obviously pursued personal power at any cost. After, then PM, David Cameron, announced a Brexit referendum in 2016 Boris prepared two very different speeches. One was a "Remain" speech if he chose to stay in the Cameron Remain camp. The other was a "Leave" speech. He chose the latter as he realised his best chance of becoming Prime Minister lay in siding with Nigel Farage and the "Leave" camp.

During the referendum campaign Boris told some real "whoppers" or plain lies. One of them was how much money the UK would save by leaving the EU. He suggested that this money could be ploughed into the National Health system. Not only were his claims untrue, it has now become apparent that leaving the EU is going to cost the UK a truly colossal amount of money, enough to seriously weaken its economy for years to come. This is quite apart from the very real risk of Scotland and Northern Ireland splitting away from the UK.

Despite all of this the Conservative Party still elected Boris as its leader and therefore PM.

11. *Jair Bolsonaro President of Brazil*

Jair Bolsonaro
(www.nationalpost.com)

Jair Bolsonaro, the new president of Brazil, is a homophobic denizen of the far right who wishes to clear more of the Amazon's rain forest to make way for more farming and presumably logging. He is not worried that *a football field amount of rainforest is being cleared every minute!*

The Amazon rainforest provides 20% of the earth's oxygen, is home to a million indigenous people and countless species of flora and fauna. Many new medicines are likely to be sourced from this rainforest. In August 2019 a record of more than 500 major separate fires, (along with hundreds of thousands of smaller ones) have been lit in the forest, an 85% increase on the previous year. Instead of employing the military to guard the forest against people lighting fires on virtual pain of death, this idiot seems to encourage the fires. He is also opposed to Brazilian workers receiving a liveable minimum wage. How did this guy get elected in the first place? What were the voters thinking?

Further evidence of Bolsonaro's total unsuitability is provided by his utterly inept and foolish response to the Corona crisis in his country. This has resulted in many thousands of deaths and millions of infections. (July 2020)

12. *Benjamin Netanyahu, longstanding Prime Minister of Israel*

Benjamin Netanyahu
(from Google images)

The last in our rogue's gallery is the present Prime Minister of Israel. Over the years he has been implicated in a number of corruption scandals but has escaped unscathed. His hard line and almost Zionist approach to the occupation of Palestinian lands and encouragement of more and more Israeli settlements on those lands, has made the prospect of a meaningful peace deal between the Palestinians and Israel all but impossible.

A realistic charter of human rights

(Jul 2013)

Preamble

Given the precarious state of life on our planet it would seem reasonable that the long-term survival of the human race is subject to some considerable doubt. Globalisation has more rapidly brought negative consequences more so than positive ones. Although circumstances would seem to be rapidly spinning out of control there is no going back. We are on a one-way journey wherever that is leading.

If we are to have any hope of overcoming these horrendous obstacles it will be necessary, in the fairly near future, to arrive at some sort of world government. That could be a UN with real teeth and power, although given its charter and the various rights of veto belonging to super powers who seldom agree, this is probably a pipe dream. A significant number of powerful nations would have to be willing to surrender most of their sovereignty. Millions die while nations and their governments follow their own agendas.

A democratic world government could only work if the bulk of humanity had sufficient education and intelligence to think both long term and fairly rather than chasing after immediate self-interest or ludicrous agendas and promises of extremist groups. The West's promotion of democracy in the Middle East is an obvious example. The moment a genuine democratic election is arranged it is often the case that a majority elect an Islamic government tending toward the extreme and the West is mortified by the results.

A world government dictatorship is undesirable as the likelihood of an enlightened leader (in the mold of the Dalai Llama) is remote. Even more so than leaders of democracies, dictators seem only interested in their own well-being and that of their immediate circle of support. Syria and North Korea are obvious cases in point.

The Dalai Lama
(from Google images)

How we are to begin in saving our species and many others is a bothersome open question. Unless we can reign in the greed and philosophical stupidity of the mega rich and the very powerful, we have little chance. The capitalist ethos of congregating more and more wealth in the hands of individuals or small groups is certainly doomed. The question is; will the survival of the human race go down with it?

A new charter of human rights will have to start from a non-capitalist standpoint. The very idea of human rights also necessarily includes the concomitant notion of human responsibilities. The idea, of rights without responsibilities, tends toward the absurd and is totally useless.

Charter of human rights

1. *All humans should respect all forms of life and live and let live wherever reasonably possible.*

2. *Every human being has the right to basic shelter, food, water and the necessary means to sustain their lives.*

3. *All people have the right to produce and raise children, (although not too many given the overpopulation of the world) in as much safety as possible. All children have the right to at least a basic education and preferably one beyond that.*

4. *People have the right to accumulate modest amounts of property and have that property protected. Such property should be subject to reasonable limits so as not to condemn others to poverty.*

5. *All humans have the right to defend themselves up to a reasonable use of force. This specifically does not include the right to bear arms. We have all seen how this amendment to the US constitution has played out. The right to bear arms actually diminishes personal safety rather than increases it.*

6. *Everybody has a right to work and an obligation to do so, health permitting, until a reasonable retirement age has been reached. Such retirees have a right to modest support for the rest of their lives. People likewise have the right to reasonable amounts of non-work time and to be compensated fairly for their work.*

7. *All humans have the right not to be exploited, economically and generally, by others. This in turn translates into the obligation not to exploit others.*

8. *All governments, from world down to local, should be secular. Human beings follow many different, and quite often competing religions. No-one, and no religion has the right to assume a monopoly on truth and hope. People can believe what they want to believe and it is impossible to stop this in any case.*

9. *All governments and large private companies should be required to be completely transparent in all their deliberations and practices. The obvious exception to this requirement is weapons-technologies and military matters. This exception is necessary to prevent such technologies falling into the hands of terrorists or criminals.*

General transparency in governance is about the only effective way to fight corruption and corruption is one of the greatest blights on humanity, blocking our way forward.

Conclusion

Unless our outdated means of coordination between nations is quickly superseded it is all but certain that our species is going to follow the dinosaurs. There is little time left to act. Violence destroys much more than it gains. The various wars are testament to this. We must find non-violent ways of disempowering those who presently run this world, and are either possessed by greed and stupidity or else hamstrung by that of others. It could be argued that Barrack Obama is one of the most enlightened presidents in US history but is hamstrung by the realities of the power and wealth cliques that lie behind him. He may possibly even believe personally that Julian Assange, Bradley Manning and Edward Snowden are right deep down. However, there is no way he could say that or exonerate them without risking a very likely assassination of himself. His position prohibits him from making many decisions and choices that he may otherwise like to make.

The only way forward is for each individual to do what he or she can to follow a path of enlightenment and fight greed and stupidity at every turn, on every level!

The Global Corona virus pandemic and its aftermath – What will follow?

The most frightening aspects of this pandemic are the myriad unknowns. The virus is spreading more rapidly than expected and it appears to be gaining more virulence. More people are dying, including those in their prime.

I can see two possibilities.

1. *We are faced with a 1930's-style Great Depression, coupled with more deaths than from the 1918 Spanish flu. This is the better scenario.*

2. *The second one is indeed terrifying. A total breakdown of the world's economic and social system, coupled with a death rate exceeding that of the great plagues or black death. This scenario would lead to complete anarchy and all the Doomsday preppers would feel completely vindicated.*

Certainly, the wealthy and powerful elites (often referred to as Illuminati) would do their level best to preserve their wealth and power and try to reset the world economic order in such a way that it would be the ordinary people who would lose their savings and suffer massive pain. This would be a type of Debt Jubilee where the slate is wiped clean and everybody starts again, (the poor and the middle class of course being the losers). These elites with their foolish debt-fuelled economic model created the mess that we now find ourselves in but they don't want to pay for it. The ordinary folk will!

However, if everything sufficiently crashes and dissolves into dust the elites may simply not be able to push the reset button. Chaos and anarchy everywhere would create an uncontrollable world. Every cloud has a semblance of a silver lining though. A massive cull of the human race, say the removal of 5 or 6 billion people, would allow the planet to have a reset. Abnormal climate change would become a thing of the past and millions of other species would have a brighter future. Assuming the surviving portion of humanity learned from their past mistakes and dramatically cut down on greed, stupidity and fear, the human race could then prosper in a sustainable way. This is a huge "IF" and in all probability the same mistakes would lead to the disastrous cycle beginning again.

The possible causes of the Corona virus and their implication for geopolitics

Amongst the disinformation spread on the Internet are claims, fostered by the Chinese government, that the virus was deliberately started and spread by the USA. Such claims are simply ludicrous. Then there is the official line from China that the virus began in a food market in Wuhan. This is possible but somewhat unlikely. The Chinese government has a biological warfare unit in Wuhan! It also has one in Beijing where the SARS virus began.

What is more likely is that the Wuhan virus was an experimental one being worked on and accidently released. Some Indian scientists claimed that this virus appears to be a standard Corona one spliced with elements of HIV and Ebola. This may be just speculative but who knows? The Chinese government arrested the doctor who first raised the alarm and he later died from the virus. Not only that, but they deliberately delayed reporting the outbreak to the World Health Organisation, although it was just before Chinese New Year when most of China's population was on the move. WHO appears to be scared of China and commended its efforts when it should have condemned them. China's government is opaque at best and truth telling is not its strong point.

At this time hundreds of thousands of Chinese headed into Italy, which signed up to the One Belt One Road project. The results are plain for all to see. Xi Jinping has long held a fascination with, and desire for power, both for himself and for China. He is determined that China should be the one and only global power, at all costs. Only a few weeks ago he was beginning to lose face in Hong Kong as the protests there showed no sign of abating.

The outbreak of the virus was a godsend for him as the demonstrations had to suddenly stop. This was suspiciously convenient. Then as the pandemic began to grip China a vague possibility emerged that the Communist Party might lose its hold on power. Two months after the outbreak, Xi turned up in Wuhan, wearing a face mask and standing behind glass. In the streets below there were a few stooges clapping him and numbers of angry people shouting defiance.

Now, if their government is to be believed, they have contained the outbreak via draconian measures and everything will soon return to normal. Then there is the added bonus that they will have broken most of the power of the West. Xi is smiling from his face to his arse.

There is also the possibility that the COVID19 virus was a deliberate biological warfare attack. I doubt that China's government cares that, in the process, it killed several thousand, or however many, of its own people. This outbreak has put China in the box seat to rule the world. That thought in itself is terrifying.

If, however, proof of a deliberate biological attack by China appears then, to coin a phrase, "It will be on for young and old!"

Retaliation from the West, particularly the USA, would be a certainty; tit for tat biological strikes or nukes, who knows? I could easily imagine Donald Trump itching to push the button. In such a scenario I think the US military would actually carry out his order!

Whichever way you look at it, Xi Jinping's China is a pariah!

Australia and the PRC Chinese Diaspora

Scott Morrison
(from Google images)

The spat between the Australian government and that of China's CCP is well known by now. However, it is only recently that Australia's PM, Scott Morrison, announced that Australia would grant students from Hong Kong a five-year extension to their visas in the wake of China's new national security law. In addition, Australia is considering granting humanitarian visas for those pro-democracy leaders who are now in serious danger.

Xi Jinping
(from Google images)

Unsurprisingly, the government of Xi Jinping is less than happy with this. While commenting on Scott Morrison's announcement, federal Labor senator, Penny Wong stated that this move couldn't compare with the late Bob Hawke's sudden granting of permanent residence visas to Chinese students who were in Australia in 1989 at the time of the Tian'anmen Square massacre.

Penny Wong
(from Google images)

Bob Hawke
(from Google images)

What many people fail to understand is that the Chinese government did not want these students to return as they probably knew about the massacre and would spread the news. Those same students, if they had returned to China and not undertaken any protests, would have had nothing to fear. While not denying his earlier achievements, the tears that the then PM, Bob Hawke, shed would prove to be very expensive ones.

We have no idea how many of the students in Australia at that time were pro-democracy. However, I have a friend whose father was a high ranking official in the CCP and she was sent to Australia to spy on pro-democracy students. She said this herself.

Gerry Hand
(from Google images)

A year or two later, the then-Minister of Immigration, Gerry Hand, appeared on television and was asked by an interviewer if Australia's family reunion policy, coupled with the grant of permanent residence visas to the roughly 20,000 students who were in the country in 1989, would mean that 300,000 additional immigrants would arrive over the next ten years. Mr Hand replied, "Yes," a very forthright answer from a politician. Three days later he was no longer Immigration Minister.

While Bob Hawke had not done anything illegal, in hindsight it would seem that he had accepted some kind of implied quid pro quo from the Chinese government. This became apparent when, not long after he had left politics, Hawke became a highly paid consultant to the Chinese government. This was the very same government that had committed the 1989 massacre. What a reversal of sentiment!

I saw Bob Hawke, in the early 2000s, on television trying to convince the Aboriginal traditional owners of land in the Northern Territory to accept spent uranium waste from China in return for financial incentives. In the years since then a large pro-CCP Chinese diaspora has emerged in Australia. They have often clashed with Hong Kong students during demonstrations.

Let's hope the present Australian government is much more careful about the granting of visas to the current Hong Kong students. We don't want any more pro-Beijing students sneaking in. I think the current government will be much more circumspect than the Hawke government was. Additionally, we can be sure that Xi Jinping's government will not be offering any "quid pro quos."

The Expansion of China and the rise of Covid-19 virus

(July 2020)

While the exact origins of the current pandemic remain a little murky it is clear that the CCP (Chinese Communist Party) of China under Xi Jinping are absolutely committed to increasing that country's expansion and power by any means possible. As the world is preoccupied with the virus and what to do about it, China is ramping up its aggression towards other nations like there is no tomorrow. Common sense, fair play and genuine diplomacy have been tossed out the window.

Top leaders of the CCP (china.org.cn)
(from Google images)

Presented with any action, statement or communication it doesn't like, the spokespeople for the CCP respond with classic twisted logic that would make any sophist proud. Almost anything that you might think of is claimed as an internal Chinese matter. Therefore, other countries should simply butt out. According to these officials, the complaints of Britain, and any other country, over the introduction of the new all-encompassing and vague security law in Hong Kong are totally unreasonable and a gross intrusion into China's internal affairs. Never mind the fact that China has trashed the formal agreement with the UK of one country, two systems that was solemnly promised for 50 years, beginning in 1997. The agreement didn't even make it to the half-way point.

Threats of economic punishment and the use of military force often spill from the mouths of the CCP. To date, only economic actions, along with arbitrary quasi legal detentions of foreign citizens, (such as the fate of two Canadians after the arrest of a Huawei executive in Canada) have occurred. Threats of direct military action have so far been reserved for the island state of Taiwan.

The CCP has bullied the rest of the world into accepting its claim that Taiwan is an integral part of China for years, despite the fact that Taiwan has its own government, issues its own passports and has its own military. Its athletes have been forced to compete in Olympics under the name of Chinese Taipei. Airlines around the world have been pressured into listing flight destinations as Taipei, China. Many have acceded to these demands out of fear of losing mainland China flights.

A brief history of Taiwan

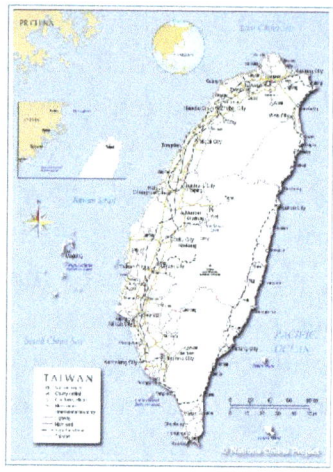

Map of Taiwan
(nationsonline.org)

The CCP and its online trolls love to distort history. Although it is true that both PRC China and Taiwan ROC claimed each other's territory, for years Taiwan was not historically part of China. After the civil war in China concluded in 1949, the Nationalists under Chiang Kai-shek fled to Taiwan, angering many of that island's inhabitants. Dreaming of a return to the mainland the Nationalists (or KMT) claimed that they had the right to rule over all China. Taiwan ROC was the rump that was left of the Republic of China. In effect, mainland China was a breakaway region of the ROC having begun as an illegal insurgency.

Returning to the history, the indigenous folk of Taiwan were a native group akin to Malays and other dark-skinned peoples. They were not ethnically Chinese. The first group of foreigners to occupy the island were the Dutch who called it Formosa (beautiful island). They arrived in the early seventeenth century and stayed for almost a hundred years. During the late seventeenth century Chinese traders from Fujian and Guangdong began to arrive and settle.

The Qing dynasty sent an army to Taiwan in 1683 and annexed the island. Taiwan was a part of China until the first Sino-Japanese war, when the Qing dynasty ceded it to Japan in 1895. Japan ruled the island until 1945 when it was returned to the Chinese Nationalists after WWII ended. The Nationalist forces fled to Taiwan in 1949 after losing the civil war. Their forces had borne more of the fighting against the Japanese than the Communists had and were therefore weakened, contributing to their defeat.

It is a fact that the British ruled over Hong Kong for a longer period of time than China ruled Taiwan. The New Territories were leased from China but Victoria Island and Kowloon were ceded to Britain in 1842 following the first Opium war. Yet nobody claims that Hong Kong was not historically part of China. Using the logic of truth and historical fact Taiwan is not an integral part of China. Quite apart from historical facts, why should the majority of people be forced to accept the authoritarianism of the PRC? Likewise, why should Taiwan's 25 million people be compelled to join authoritarian China when it is clear that the overwhelming majority of them do not want to.

Tsai Ing-Wen, the president of Taiwan, has very eloquently and rationally explained Taiwan's position. The criminal and rogue regime of Xi Jing ignores this common sense and continues its quest to dominate as much of the world as it can.

Tsai Ing-Wen
(Wikipedia)

The emergence of the Corona virus

Despite some claims that evidence of Covid-19 has been found in Europe a year or more earlier, (the research is not solid enough to be accepted) it is all but certain that the virus did indeed first emerge in Wuhan, China late last year. Reports within China began in November 2019. Initially, the Chinese government tried to completely suppress any information about it and sanctioned the doctors who reported it in the first place, one of whom later died from the disease.

It seems more than likely that the Beijing government was to some extent aware of the danger the virus posed by December 2019. It began the lockdown of Wuhan on 23 January 2020 and soon extended lockdowns over much of China. Three flights a week from Wuhan, capital of Hubei province, to Milan continued until Italy suspended them on 31 January. The Beijing government banned all flights between Hubei province and the rest of China on 23 January in an apparent effort to reign in the outbreak domestically. Further harsh lockdowns followed in many regions. Yet it happily allowed international flights to continue until the end of March. By that time this new plague had been fully unleashed on the world.

Taiwan health officials informed the World Health Organisation (WHO) of the dangers of this virus back in December, 2019 but senior officials at the WHO refused to even listen. Canadian Dr Bruce Aylward, a senior adviser the WHO, when interviewed by Yvonne Tong of Hong Kong's RTHK about why Taiwan's warning was not acknowledged, replied: "Well, we've already talked about China. And when you look across all the different areas of China, they've actually all done quite a good job." and then apparently cut off the video interview link.

Dr Tedros
(guardian.com)

The head of the WHO, Dr Tedros, was praising Beijing's response to the virus and downplaying its seriousness for quite a while. It was only some months later that he was warning the world to take the virus much more seriously. By this time the pandemic was totally obvious. It would certainly appear that the PRC government pressured the WHO to ignore the seriousness of Covid-19 until the contagion had well and truly spread.

Taiwan is probably the country in the word that has had the most successful response to the virus with few cases and hardly any deaths. It achieved this without even imposing lockdowns apart from the isolation and monitoring of returned travellers. Taiwan reacted earlier than anybody else to the virus by ignoring what China and the WHO were saying and implementing sensible measures such as mask wearing and contact tracing.

When Australia's PM, Scott Morrison, announced the banning of arrivals from China and advised Australians not to travel there on 1 February, the Beijing government complained bitterly. It certainly appears that it wished the virus to spread as far as possible globally.

A purely natural virus or not?

Although many experts and China itself claim that the virus originated in a Wuhan wet market, (when it is not claiming that the virus came from the USA) one has to wonder. It is a fact that a number of countries are researching viruses under the guise of looking for medical breakthroughs. It is more than likely that some of them are researching biological weapons although these are outlawed under the Geneva Convention.

As time has gone on the awful effects of this virus are becoming more apparent. Not only does it cause injury to the lungs but can also cause strokes, heart attacks and damage to the brain. Additionally, there are long term effects emerging amongst some survivors, which include chronic pain. I find it difficult to believe that such a complex virus could simply come from nature. More likely, I suspect, this is a virus that has been tweaked in a laboratory. Wuhan has one such lab amongst a number in China. Whether the release of the virus was deliberate or accidental is a matter of pure conjecture.

The People's Republic of China has obviously caused the spread of this Corona virus to other parts of the world such that it has become a global pandemic, with massive loss of life and inestimable economic damage. It is continuing to use the pandemic as an ideal opportunity to increase its power and aggressive expansion.

The outrageous imposition of the security law in Hong Kong is a prime example. Even before the outbreak of the pandemic, China was economically bullying small countries in the Pacific and Africa by seemingly bribing their political leaders to accept dubious loans under the One belt, One Road program and then threatening to take over parts of their infrastructure if they are unable to repay these loans. A few countries have experienced just such a result. Sri Lanka is one of them.

Another example of Chinese expansionism is the illegal annexation of parts of the South China Sea and the construction of military bases on artificial islands created there. Another one is the attack on Indian troops in 2020, while trying to expand over the line of control that separates the two countries.

China continues its march toward world domination and the emergence of the Corona virus is just another battleground. Xi Jinping and the CCP have no interest in ethics or real diplomacy. They are only interested in power and money. Any reasonable actions they have performed are generally the result of having been compelled to take such, again by the exercise of power (economic or other) on the part of others.

Essays about Humanity and Lifestyle

This next section deals with commentary on the human race which, although some of it may have political ramifications, deserves its own place in the sun.

(Jul 2013)

The Singularity.

Prof. Vernor Vinge
(en.wikipedia.org)

Every day millions of people have the task of constantly learning new things merely to be able to perform their employment duties properly.

It is undoubtedly true that the task of keeping up with constant changes is becoming more and more demanding as well as expensive. The rate of change in the modern world is increasing exponentially. Just to be able to cope with our work and our lives in general, we will have to increasingly learn much more.

Given the exponential rate of change the human race is going to reach a point where we are simply unable to learn and remember the amount of information that we will need to in order to survive. Professor Vernor Vinge coined the phrase, "the singularity." The singularity is that point when the rate of change against the time axis goes off the chart. There is simply no way of stopping or slowing down this exponential rate of change. Perhaps the only solution will lie in humans becoming androids, with powerful computer chips embedded in their brains.

A Metaphor for Humanity

(Feb 2018)

(from Google images)

Humanity's progress through the ages could be described as a very powerful automobile with very poor steering. Technologically, humankind has become somewhat advanced. Science and medicine are progressing at a pace. Yet with each technological advance, Man has employed it to produce more sophisticated capacity for killing, albeit at a huge economic cost.

Likewise, although we are grateful for advances in medicine, there has been insufficient consideration given to the problems of ever-increasing overpopulation and an ever-increasing proportion of elderly people in those populations as life expectancy increases.

Following the dollar trail gives a great insight into what our species as a whole considers really important. Financial investment and incentives are thrown at science and technology, while almost no resources are directed towards philosophy and the humanities. Philosophy can be considered as the steering of our metaphorical vehicle, whereas science and technology equate to the power of the engine.

What is the value or point of ever-increasing speed and power without adequate thought being given to the direction of travel? The questions of the environment, society and ultimately even the economy have been subjugated to the pursuit of power. While science and technology certainly increase the scope and depth of our knowledge, without accompanying philosophical considerations they do little to add to our wisdom.

Testosterone and Youth

(Aug 2013)

Have you ever wondered why so many of our youth come to violent ends? Many die in car accidents and others perish in needless social violence, often fuelled by drugs and alcohol.

As part of the growing process it seems certain that risk taking, particularly amongst young males but also to a much lesser extent among females, is here to stay. Why? It would appear that such behaviour, although undesirable, is a part of the human condition. After the Second World War there was much less deliberate risk-taking by youth than is the case today. The reason is simple: the youth then, had totally got this behaviour out of their systems because they were exposed to massive risks during the war. Those that survived had moved past that stage of development.

The question today is: "How do we accommodate this natural but undesirable behaviour in our current world?" I would suggest that teens who feel this primal urge, be encouraged to undertake dangerous but socially beneficial work as charity workers in war zones or places that are simply too dangerous to attract most people. In that way the "danger urge" of youth is spent while improving the world rather than detracting from it.

Healthy attitudes to sex go a long way towards a healthy society

So many human social problems have their origins in sexual matters.

(Oct 2015)

Mental illness is an ever-expanding scourge of human society and much mental illness stems from sexual problems. Quite often, the problems a person has in relating to others originate from sexual issues. Without a secure, non-threatening childhood and a reasonably smooth passage through the teenage years, a person can find him or herself confused and angry, although this state may not be entirely on a conscious level.

The consequences of such a state can manifest themselves as a "bomb waiting to explode." It is small wonder then that viciously violent crazies, such as those who seem to make up the Islamic State gang, have enshrined sexual crimes into their operational program. Female prisoners from conquered areas are, all too often, forced into sexual slavery.

Without appeals to sexual opportunity, despite supporting a religion that has very strict views about relations between the sexes, how would ISIS, ISIL etc. attract so many Jihardis to their cause?

(from Google images)

Regardless of sexual mores promoted by various religions or even by total libertinism, a society must establish clear ideas of appropriate family relationships and a lucid understanding of appropriate sexual and non-sexual relations. While not denying the existence of physical or sexual desire, a healthy society promotes respect for the rights of all individuals and discourages the view that men or women can ONLY be sex objects. This respect and understanding are fundamental to healthy relationships. I am not denying the role of (voluntary) prostitution in handling various and overwhelming physical needs outside of a normal relationship. Yet it is vital for each of the sexes to view their counterparts of the opposite sex as people with thoughts, ideas and feelings.

(from Google images)

What do the predominantly male Jihardis see when they imagine women? Do they see their own women dressed in burkas as the epitome of the fair sex or do they fantasise about scantily clad women as objects of desire? It is easy to see that this dichotomy is not likely to promote healthy human relationships.

(from Google images)

A balanced, fair and reasonable view about sex is vital for healthy human societies. Mass education on these points will reduce instances of paedophilia, incest and child sexual abuse. Sexuality gone wrong is one of the greatest causes of human suffering known. Sometimes it takes years to emerge and bursts forth in the strangest of ways.

When considering matters religious and political, it is absolutely vital that whatever creed a person follows promotes healthy attitudes towards sex. Without sex a species quickly dies. With inappropriate or disturbed sex, the seeds of a society's destruction are quickly sown. Globalisation means that the evils of one locale rapidly spread to another.

The World spends more of its Scarce Resources on prolonging the lives of the frail elderly, many of whom are in a terminal condition, than it does in promoting the health of babies and young children.

Why is this absurd situation allowed to happen?

(Feb 2016)

In most of the world's countries more money is spent on prolonging the lives of the elderly than in promoting the health of their greatest resource: children. The situation reaches the height of absurdity in the case of dementia patients. The resources required to provide daily care for these people are considerable. Especially for those in the final stages, there is no quality of life and it is difficult to imagine that they could actually wish to remain alive.

I have personally experienced both ends of this medical-resources scandal in Australia.

Expensive care of the elderly when no quality of life remains.

My father, Peter Spencer, with his granddaughter, Claire.

This was probably not long after his dementia began.

Firstly, my own father died in 2015 after a long battle with vascular dementia, at the age of almost 91. The last three years of his life were spent in a high care nursing home and I would candidly assert that he did not have a good quality of life for several years before that. For the three years before he entered the nursing facility, my sister lived in his house and acted as his carer. By 2012 he had deteriorated to the point where she could no longer cope.

Unfortunately, my father had not made any sort of advanced health care directive so the nursing home was legally obliged to keep him alive for as long as reasonably possible. During the three years he was resident in the home I had occasion to see the detail of medical tests and treatments he had been receiving. The number and estimated costs thereof were truly staggering. My dad was a truly kind and wonderful person. However, by this time, his essence had largely gone.

My father in his nursing home

As a self-funded retiree, it was my father's own money that paid for his care in the facility. In addition, he was required to pay a similar amount in the form of government taxes. However, the situation is completely different for those on the aged pension. Eighty-five percent of their pension is taken for their keep in nursing homes. The rest of the considerable cost is borne by the public purse and hence the tax payer.

Fewer resources are directed at the health and welfare of babies and young children.

Again, my understanding of this side of the equation is from my personal experience. My little daughter, Claire, died on 6 June 2008 from no known cause. She simply went to sleep and didn't wake up. This was ten days before her second birthday. This phenomenon is known as SUDC (Sudden Unexplained Death in Childhood – website is www.sudc.org) and is applied to children, over one year of age, who die this way. It is much rarer than SIDS.

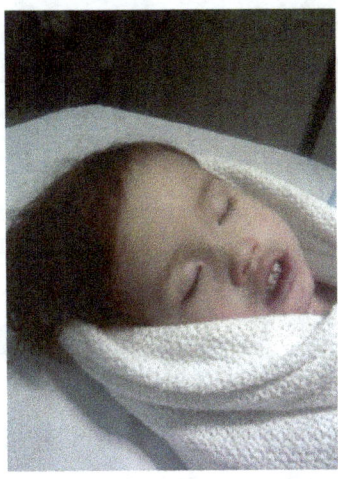

Claire

I don't wish to digress from the topic too much but Claire was a totally gorgeous spirit. Even before she could walk, she would willingly share her toys with other children and her food with the dog. Later, she would walk up to the lonely and dispossessed, and brighten their day. I had never seen such a shining light before in my entire life.

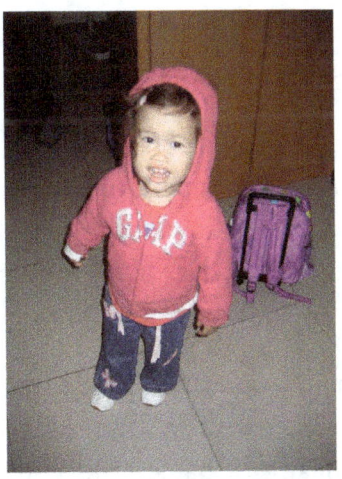

Claire

Two months before she passed away, Claire experienced four febrile convulsions in a 12-hour period. During the first one she stopped breathing for 30 seconds. She was taken by ambulance to a private hospital. They assured us that febrile convulsions were harmless and sent her home with instructions that she be given Panadol to lower her temperature. Late that evening, she had another minor convulsion and then another major one. Again, we called an ambulance. This time we took her to the public hospital on the Gold Coast in Queensland, where we live.

We were placed in a corner and left for several hours. Then, in front of a group of doctors, she suffered a major convulsion. Finally, her situation was taken seriously and she was admitted to the Children's Ward for 24 hours. We asked what tests could be performed to discover the cause of the convulsions and what could then be done. The doctors suggested that because of her age she wouldn't be able to keep still enough for an MRI. To this day I still don't know if their reluctance to perform any tests was due to the question of financial cost. We even offered to pay for any tests but none (apart from simple blood tests) were offered.

Her febrile convulsions were ascribed to a high temperature caused by an unknown virus.

After 24 hours in hospital, Claire was discharged and we were given instructions to monitor her temperature and judiciously administer child doses of Panadol. We followed this advice and all was well for a while. Then on that fateful day, two months later, Claire died in her sleep.

My wife and I can't help wondering if the situation would have been any different had the amount of resources expended on the elderly been applied to the health of babies and young children. Statistics from around the world will bear out the fact that the expenditure on prolonging the lives of the elderly is much greater than that devoted to the health of young children! Although I am somewhat elderly myself, I see this situation as a gross travesty of natural justice.

A more complete account of her life is given in my book, "Waiting for A Miracle – Life in the Dead Zone" available in either eBook or printed form on Amazon.

Early Demise for the Elderly The Ugly side of the Future

(Feb 2015)

(from Google images)

In late 2013 China announced that it was relaxing the one child policy. Despite the fact that this policy was an attempt at preventing critical overpopulation, the Chinese government is relaxing it because they already have too many old people in their society. With not enough young workers, who will pay to keep the elderly? You are probably right when you gasp, "No-one!" This would-be solution is obviously a very short-term fix.

Climate change is a bad enough problem but at least it can be mentioned! The question of how to deal with the elderly is a problem that, around the world, politicians won't touch. The reason is that, if they were honest, it would cause panic amongst the not-so-young.

My prediction is probably as correct as it is chilling: within ten years or so, around the globe, (short of a pandemic that reduces the world's population by at least half and particularly hits the elderly), euthanasia will go from being illegal to compulsory. The rich and powerful are not going to pay to keep the "dead wood" alive. The future for them looks ugly and bleak.

Pile of skulls and bones
(from Google images)

It is simply going to be impossible to keep ever increasing numbers of very elderly people, the majority of whom have dementia, in nursing homes alive. Forgetting for the moment the miserable quality of their lives, there isn't the money, the resources, nor the numbers of young people to act as nurses and carers, to sustain this ridiculous situation much longer. It costs more than twice as much to keep a person with dementia alive as it does to save a critically ill baby.

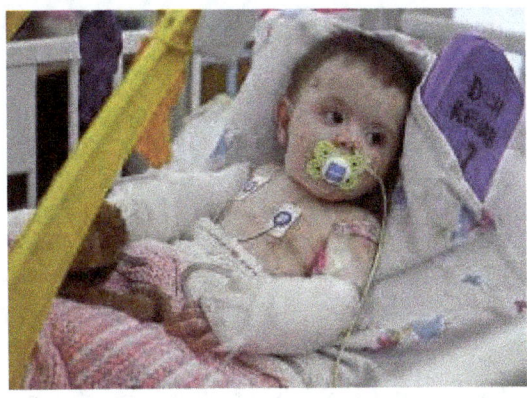

baby girl
(from Google images)

Within ten years or so I predict that euthanasia will go from being illegal in most countries to compulsory for those who are no longer independent or vaguely productive. Some politicians and community leaders vehemently argue that human life must be preserved as long as possible no matter what the cost.

Nonetheless, more intelligent and logical leaders and forces in the world are most likely already working on this problem. It goes without saying that the world of the near future will make Hitler look like a boy scout. (In a way, albeit a cruel one, that leader did try to prevent some of the disasters that are now swamping the world). I strongly suspect that the global plan for dealing with the problem of the elderly will follow these steps; firstly euthanise all residents of nursing homes with dementia, secondly get rid of the rest of the residents of nursing homes, thirdly remove all retirees (apart from the wealthy and powerful) and lastly the extermination of the long-term unemployed.

It is already possible that certain scientists around the world are attempting to develop and produce viruses that will only target the elderly. Governments in Australia will, in all probability, merely make it too expensive for the elderly to receive any medical attention.

The future for the elderly is scary, ugly and horrible but I fear, short of a natural pandemic that wipes out more than half of mankind, it cannot be avoided.

Buddhism and Christianity

(Mar 2015)

Buddhism has its origins in the teachings of the Buddha who lived several hundred years before Christ. Perhaps the most striking of Buddha's teachings were his desire to overcome suffering and his discovery of the middle way; it is not necessary to deny the needs of the flesh in order to achieve spiritual enlightenment.

To be accurate, it should be mentioned that this religion shares some common background and concepts with Hinduism and both religions were influenced by the ideas of the more ancient tantric practice of Yoga. Today, Buddhism has several branches but all of which promote a common respect for all living creatures. Buddhism does not single out mankind as the only significant and worthy life form. In its great precept of overcoming suffering, Buddhism encourages vegetarianism and has always disavowed violence.

Christianity shares a common historical antecedent with both Islam and Judaism. That common origin flows through the teachings of the Old Testament; the Torah and the Koran. Christianity was essentially a dramatic revision of all Judaic teaching that had occurred before the time of Christ.

Christ's teachings, while maintaining the fundamental framework of the Old Testament scriptures, offered something else, something fundamentally different from Judaism and from the later teachings of Mohammed. Jesus preached a much "softer" view of the world. Animals had a respected place in it and the precepts of love and mercy assumed a much greater importance than those of simple obedience and punishment for transgressors.

Given the inherited background of Christianity, how and where did Jesus come by his completely radical ideas? It is probably fair to say that, in many respects, his ideas were fundamentally different from and more radical than those of Judaism or the later Islam. It is quite possible that Jesus Christ was heavily influenced by Buddhist teachings as the journey from Palestine to India was not a huge one, even in ancient times.

Tobacco taxes, poverty and organised crime

(Jan 2019)

Scott Morrison PM
(from Google images)

Richard Dinatale leader of the Greens
(from Google images)

While nobody would argue that smoking is healthy or that it shouldn't be discouraged, the entire Australian federal parliament is guilty of the unintended and horrendous consequences of the current "tax them till death" policy. Australia's approach to this issue not only makes us the laughing stock of the world but also causes massive harm to our own society. Various political parties and groups have factored in to projected revenues these draconian tax levels.

The hypocrisy is evident to anyone with half a brain. Are "Quit Smoking" aids free? Of course not!

The Negative consequences of this stupid policy

There are many people, who cannot or will not (for various reasons) quit. Quite often these people are amongst the poorest in our community. This reads as "children without shoes or enough to eat."

Tobacco products are so expensive in Oz that smokers drag their fags until the very end, thus consuming more tar and poisons. The mentally ill tend to smoke and it is always much harder for them to quit than for the general population. My own sister suffers from bipolar type 1, is a pensioner and one of her doctors told her not to try to quit as it would increase her stress levels and thus her illness. I, myself suffer from severe depression and OCD. I can't see a way to quitting either.

Organised crime is laughing all the way to the bank. This policy is expanding and enabling the reach of organised-crime networks. Tobacco is now more expensive than marijuana or meth amphetamine ("ice)." Troubled youth, who may have previously resorted to smoking are now taking the drug ice, which is far more dangerous for both the individual and society as a whole.

Alternatives

There are many ways to discourage smoking without targeting the extremely vulnerable. It is possible to set an age for purchase of smoking products (demanding ID) and raising it every year. That should assist in keeping the young from the evil habit. Progressive reductions in public areas where smoking is allowed can also help.

An example of a sensible tobacco policy that I am familiar with, springs to mind. In Taiwan the rate of smoking amongst the young is much lower than that in Oz. Their campaigns against smoking have become a cultural norm. Yet they do not target the vulnerable sections of their society such as the hopelessly addicted elderly, the mentally ill (my brother-in-law in Taiwan is battling schizophrenia fairly successfully, he smokes and is a low-income earner).

The Future.

Will any of our parliamentary leaders have the courage to try to solve this problem and set tobacco taxes at reasonable and sensible levels? I can only hope so but I doubt it! Australia is heading for third world status in a rush in all areas but one: tobacco prices!

Want to be rich for a day or a month?

How to experience the sensation of being wealthy

(Feb 2015)

[pininterest.com]

Most of us complain from time to time that we are having a tough go of it financially in this life. We may occasionally glance at the trappings of wealth displayed by others with a hint of wistful longing. Almost all of us, at some time or other, have remarked that we would like to be rich for a week or so just to see what the experience is like.

The good news is that wealth is relative. If you were a millionaire living in a village entirely populated, apart from yourself, with billionaires you would undoubtedly feel impoverished. The sensation of feeling abundantly wealthy in a material sense derives from comparisons with others. Therefore, it is perfectly possible for an ordinary person to temporarily experience a life of relative wealth.

[engineeredlifestyles.org]

The way to do this is to take a vacation to another country that has a much lower standard of living and a favourable exchange rate for one's home currency. Quite apart from areas of natural, social and cultural interest, such a destination will instantly offer the traveller a personal situation of newfound riches. Goods and services that hitherto were beyond reach are now easily attainable. The visitor can enjoy upmarket accommodation, gourmet restaurants, stunning entertainment and the purchase of luxury goods at bargain rates.

If a little voice in your head cried, "There must be a catch!" you are right. In this land, with a much lower standard of living, you may find that standards of personal security and safety are much lower than what you are used to, but not necessarily so. Perhaps the risk of theft or even personal attack is greater in this destination. In any case this would be a valid portion of the experience of being rich. In most nations the wealthy find it necessary to protect their possessions and even their personal safety with more rigorous security than do the rest of us.

[aljazeera.com]

[thehackernews.com]

Of course, the lucky, or well-researched traveller who finds a low-cost destination with little crime risk is much more likely to have a thoroughly enjoyable holiday. However your vacation pans out you will have had the experience of being rich for a day, a week or a month! No longer will you have to exclaim in conversations at dinner parties, "I'd just like to try being rich!"

Notes about my first novel, "Brownout – 666: The Compelling Inside Story of a Misguided Life in the Sex and Drug Trade and the real meaning of the Swastika."

The third and final section of this book includes a number of posts about the background of my novel. Many of its themes relate to some of the posts in the preceding two sections, which is why I think it may interest you.

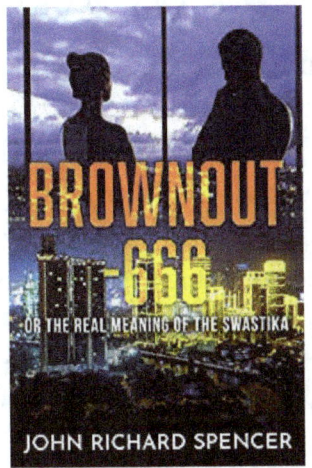

The author

(Dec 2018)

Why I wrote this novel

Although I was teaching at Cromer High School as the cold case disappearance of Lynette Dawson and the male teacher and schoolgirl sex rings were unfolding, and although I had first heard of the allegations of murder in the 1990's, this intriguing case has nothing directly to do with my reasons for penning this tale.

In fact, the only and indirect reference to Cromer High in my story was somewhat a matter of chance. Much of my novel, "Brownout-666: or the real meaning of the swastika," is based on real events. I could have written part of the story as a nonfiction work but, (aside from the constant danger of being sued for liable or defamation), I also wanted to include my take on what is happening to human society and its disastrous consequences around the world. Political inaction on climate change, corruption, greed and abject stupidity, (along with short sightedness on many levels) have all long concerned me.

In addition, I wanted to explore exploitative sexuality along with the passion of Eros and romantic love – hence the graphic sex scenes. In Australia of the 1970s and 1980s many young men were sexually frustrated. That, in addition to the prevailing culture of the time, probably caused a sexually exploitative and conquest attitude amongst many males. It is these themes that are common to "The Teacher's Pet" podcast and my novel.
https://www.youtube.com/watch?v=2XzhquLFYGI

The Political and Social thought of John Richard Spencer

Cory Aquino
(from Google images)

The word "Brownout" appears many times and has meaning on numerous levels. When I lived in the Philippines in the late 80s and early 90s, I told people that one day I would write a book called "Brownout." Brownouts (or the sudden cutting of electricity supply) were ubiquitous during my sojourns in that country. On another level the term has metaphorical meaning: cultural clash or an inability to deal with problems in a logical and systematic way is just like the dying of the light. Many of the problems that I experienced in the Philippines, including the massive corruption, exist everywhere but in more subtle forms.
https://www.youtube.com/watch?v=g1CWJjVeJuI

Truth and justice are almost impossible to achieve, but every year our world seems to slip further and further from those ideals. My novel is both a warning and a call to action for humanity.

Rick Daly, the central character in the novel

(Dec 2018)

The central character, Rick Daly, is a composite from many people I have known, along with some fictional elements. Portions of his makeup I have taken from myself but I would certainly disown some of the actions he undertakes during his journey of self-discovery. Some of his attributes are considerably more extreme and apparently somewhat callous, than any that my younger self, possessed.

Some of the apparently heartless actions undertaken by Rick, (such as the way he treats a drunk female passenger who can't pay the fare in his cab,) were taken from real life but not mine. His happy-go-lucky attitude during the beginning of the story and his predatory behaviour relates to many young Australian males of the seventies and eighties and in all likelihood stems from some deep sense of sexual frustration, along with a failure to fully understand women as people on many levels.

Joanne Curtis c. 1980
(expressdigest.com)

This theme is in evidence in "The Teacher's Pet" podcast and its allegations of teacher-schoolgirl sex rings at three high schools on

Sydney's northern beaches. Youngish males who were obsessed with their sexual gratification and used any available means to achieve it, were referred to repeatedly in this podcast, along with the allegations of murder against Chris Dawson who was arrested and is currently on bail.

Cromer High School c. 1979 – 1982
(frasercroastchronicle.com.au)

Cromer High School c. 1979 – 1982
(northernstar.com.au)

Rick, the product of his time, operates his life against a background of constantly wanting to "get his end in" in the most enjoyable way possible. He certainly possesses some hedonistic values at the beginning of the novel.

Fortunately, over time he learns some of the subtleties and more important values, albeit, in many cases, the hard way. He also learns about love and its pitfalls, corruption and the inescapable fact that life is not fair. By the conclusion of the story he realises just how rotten the world and its powers can be. He manages this without surrendering his interest in sex and love but, by putting everything into perspective, achieves a level of inner peace.

The other major characters in Brownout – 666

(Jan 2019)

The character of Marilyn Delgado, Rick's love interest, is largely based on that of a young woman I once employed as a secretary. Many of Marilyn's actions in the story are entirely fictional.

Typical Filipina secretary at work
(from Google images)

Marilyn is a moderately devout Catholic but remains a physical person with the usual hopes and aspirations. She is a proud Filipino but is often the victim of her own culture.

Christopher Daly, Rick's uncle, is a really a composite of people I have known. He is a highly moral man who always tries to do the right thing. His own morals often give him a weakness that makes him an easy victim of unscrupulous people and organisations.

Typical SS soldier
(from Google images)

Hans Werttenburger, is a diehard Nazi and former SS man, whose views on Hitler and WWII have changed little over the decades. I based him on SS men I met in Germany in the 1970s.

Precocious schoolgirl
(from Google images)

The Character of Alma Lopez, the 14-year-old schoolgirl, was based on a number of precocious teenagers I met over the years in the Philippines.

Typical Filipina nurse in uniform
(from Google images)

Cecilia Crisputa, was based on a qualified nurse who once worked for me as a maid.

My novel is available on Amazon in both eBook and print formats.

The minor characters in Brownout-666: or the real meaning of the swastika

(Jan 2019)

Quite obviously it would not be practicable to discuss every minor character in the novel, so I shall restrict my comments to the more important ones.

Typical Filipina bargirl
(from Google images)

Lina/Maria – the bargirl who kept her job hidden as much as possible.

Lina was actually based on a number of girls I personally knew in that "fishing" village in Northern Samar, Philippines. These girls plied their trade in Manila, Cebu or other parts of the country but pretended to have innocent jobs when they returned home. Considering the amounts of money they would send to their families, it would beggar belief that their jobs were as maids or shop assistants. Their families obviously knew but would pretend that they didn't. The money came and that was OK.

Ricardo Gordon – the mixed blood fixer

This character was formed from a number of foreigners and mixed blood people who had taken unto themselves the worst aspects of Filipino character and motivations. Hence the quote from the book that you don't trust your own mother once she sets foot in that land.

The Colonel, Major and other military men who often drank with Rick at Alfred's Kitchenette in Cebu City.

Philippine army soldiers in action
(from Google images)

These people are simply described as they actually were and are taken from real life.

The police captain, his sergeant and members of his squad.

Philippine police ready for action
(from Google images)

Apart from name changes most of the actions, including the visits to Rick's house, are simply taken from actual events. These include the Armalites stacked against the wall of his lounge room and Rick's visit to the private hospital and subsequent "arrest." Truth can indeed be stranger than fiction.

Christopher Daly's children

George, his son is a typical child who has had a difficult childhood and then goes off the rails as a teenager.

Likewise, Rebecca is a somewhat rebellious teenager but improves with growing maturity.

Elizabeth, Christopher's youngest child is based on some of the brightest and kindest children I came across during my time as a school teacher. When Elizabeth dies from meningococcal disease I, as the author, felt sorry that we had lost her.

My own young daughter, who mysteriously died from no known cause (Sudden Unexplained Death in Childhood – the website for the support organisation is www.sudc.org) just before her second birthday and is the subject of my book about grief, "Waiting for a Miracle – Life in the Dead Zone," was still alive when I wrote the initial draft of my novel. In a crazy way I wondered if my "killing" of Elizabeth had tempted fate.

The characters of the Organisation

These are mostly fictional but portions of them are from people I knew or heard about. The Organisation is a sophisticated international crime ring.

Hannah Chibber

Blonde Jewish girl
(beauty-around.com)

Hannah is the niece of a very senior Organisation member.

The Delgado family

This family is largely based on a family I personally knew in the Philippines. I hope the above background increases your desire to read this novel.

The Teacher's Pet, Chris Dawson and me

(Dec 2018)

Chris Dawson
(the morningbulletin.com.au)

Chris Dawson, Joanne Curtis & Lynnette Dawson c. 1980
(tremr.com)

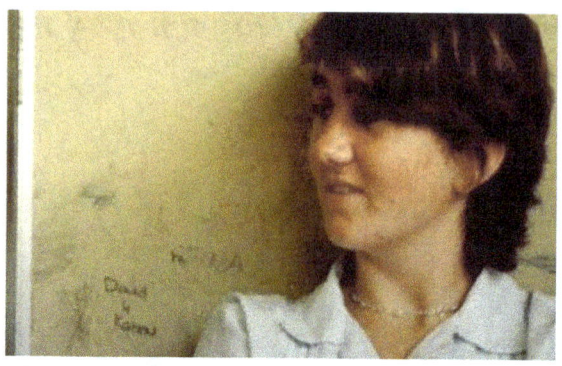

Robyn Wheeler (student c. 1980)
(dailymercury.com.au)

John Spencer, author of "Brownout-666: or the real meaning of the swastika" was a teacher at Sydney's Cromer High School between 1979 and 1981 and he personally knew many of the protagonists in this cold case probable murder and story of lust, schoolgirls, betrayal and improper sexuality that is currently grabbing headlines around the world and is the subject of The Teacher's Pet podcast by Hedley Thomas of the "The Australian" newspaper.

John's novel is largely based on true events and, while only making one indirect reference to Cromer High School, explores in depth many of the themes apparent in this podcast; including male predatory sexual behaviour from that era, changes to such attitudes over the decades and the legal ramifications thereof, older men pursuing young girls, and the particular socio/sexual problems of Australian men at that time that may have led to their hunter/conquest at-all-costs attitudes.

John's book is available on Amazon
https://amzn.to/2Mn8bHC
and from his website.
His email address is jspe3506@bigpond.net.au and his website is www.creativityandpower.com

All photographs and artworks depicted, unless otherwise attributed, are from the public domain or are owned by the author.

೫ ♦ ♦ ♦ ♦ ☏

© John Spencer 2020

www.ingramcontent.com/pod-product-compliance
Lightning Source LLC
Chambersburg PA
CBHW050318010526
44107CB00055B/2295